LIVING LIFE *in* FULL BLOOM

LIVING LIFE *in* FULL BLOOM

120 Daily Practices to Deepen
Your Passion, Creativity & Relationships

Elizabeth Murray

RODALE.

Rodale books may be purchased for business or promotional use or for special sales. For information, please write to: Special Markets Department, Rodale Inc., 733 Third Avenue, New York, NY 10017

Printed in China
Rodale Inc. makes every effort to use acid-free ♾, recycled paper ♻.

Photography by Elizabeth Murray, with the exception of:
Craig Lovell, page x; Duncan Berry, pages 30, 98, 163, 165, and 166; NASA, page 128; Anna Rainville, page 145 (top right); David Judge, pages 150, 151 (from the family's collection), 152 (middle and lower left), 152 (top right from the family's collection); Tyler Shaw, page 160 (top); Kathy Karn, page 161; Kaj Wyn Berry, page 162; Lily Yeh, page 180, and Teresa Yeh, page 181; Ana Elena Pena, page 183; Gracie Kyle, page 212.

Art and illustration by Elizabeth Murray, with the exception of calligraphy, page 121, by Thich Nhat Hanh; painting of Betty Peck, page 143, by Helen Caswell, photographed by Nancy Martin; Lita Judge, pages 151–154.

Book design by Carol Angstadt

Library of Congress Cataloging-in-Publication Data is on file with the publisher.

ISBN 978–1–62336–120–4   hardcover

Distributed to the trade by Macmillan

2   4   6   8   10   9   7   5   3   1   hardcover

We inspire and enable people to improve their lives and the world around them.
rodalebooks.com

To the patient Gardeners in my life, who planted seeds,
watered, weeded, and pruned and who opened paths that
inspired me to be both cultivated and wild

To my mother, Patricia Catherine Kilkenny Murray, who
instilled in me a love of Nature, gardens, imagination, and
creativity and who encouraged me to follow my heart and deepen
my belief in God, the Great Mystery that holds both
the vast darkness and the illuminating light

To my uncle Father Frank Murray, a Catholic priest
for more than 60 years and a loving and faithful Gardener
of souls, who served with humbleness, humility,
and good old Irish humor

To my uncle Fenton Kilkenny, who ignited a passion for
exotic travel, passed along a gift for storytelling,
and taught me to appreciate joy and diversity

And to Gerald Bol, who was a Full Bloomer

Contents

Introduction x

THE FOUR PATHWAYS...1

Explore the pathways and daily practices of the four personality archetypes—*Gardener*, *Artist*, *Lover*, and *Spirit-Weaver*—to cultivate your soul, lead you to greater purpose, expand your creativity and imagination, fall in love with life, and bring celebrations and blessing into each new day.

Gardener ...3

Ahh and Awe • Finding Wildness Within • Create Sacred Space • Welcoming the Birds • Breathe • Butterflies, Transformation, and You • Invite a Child into the Garden • Create a Fairy Mailbox • The Beauty of a Bloom • Greet the Dawn • Savor Food with Gratitude • Purposeful Happiness • The Allure of Herbs • Coming Home • One Step at a Time • Learn from Permaculture • Play Like a Child • Pollination: The Kiss of Life • Plant Seeds • Attentiveness and Patience • Awaken Your Senses • The Soil and the Soul • Eyes to the Sky • Respect the Spirit of Place • Embrace the Night • Make Generosity a Habit • Glean Wisdom from Trees • Good Vibrations • Wabi, Sabi, Suki • Water: Every Drop Precious

Artist ...37

Art Studio on the Go • Ephemeral Art • An Artist's State of Mind • Create an Artist's Journal • Radical Amazement • Celebrate Beauty • Adorn Your Body • Create Community • Clear Up Creative Clutter • Let's Dance • Remember the Six Ds • Draw Playfully • Heal through Art • Make Your Home Your Art • Imagine • Inspiration • Lose Yourself to Find Your Self • Welcome Your Muse • The Courage to Express • Flowers as Art • Finding Your Song • Nature as Your Mentor • Notice, Appreciate, Discern • Paint • Try Photography • Remember to Play • Writing Poetry • Taking the Leap • Tell a Story • Textiles for Art and Healing

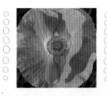

Lover ...71

Living on Purpose • Find Your Passions • Honor Your Ancestors • Learn from Animals • Nurture the Children • Embrace Your Elders • Cherish Your Friendships • Give Thanks • Live in Loving Kindness • Fall in Love with Nature • This Moment Only Once • Be a Fierce Warrior • What You Love • Make Commitments • Communication That Matters • Courage and Encouragement • Be Curious • Depth and Clarity • Treasure Your Family • Be Flexible in Mind and Body • Be Authentic • Forgive to Live • Cultivate Intimacy • Deep Listening • Find Your Spirit • Passion for Place • Dare to Serve • Cultivate Sufficiency • Let In Vulnerability • The Way of the Lover

Spirit-Weaver ...105

The Importance of Activism • Becoming a Peach • Beginning Anew • Make Blessings • Create Celebration and Rituals • Find Compassion for Yourself • Of Death and Impermanence • Listen to Your Dreams • The Joy of Giving • Know Your Happiness • Five Universal Forces • The Healing Power of Humor • Trust Your Intuition • Leadership • Following the Light • Open to Being the Lotus • Meditation and Prayer • Find a Mentor • Presence of Mind • The Big Picture • Observe Your Sabbath • The Sound of Silence • A Gift to Be Simple • Stewardship • From Deep within Your Soul • Find Your Tribe • All Kinds of Time • Following Your Calling • Wisdom Keepers • Zen Sticky Notes

FULL BLOOMERS ...141

Meet inspiring individuals who exemplify a life lived in Full Bloom and who work in partnership with local communities and international organizations focused on people, Nature, and service.

BETTY PECK   LITA JUDGE   DAVID BAUM AND TERRY REEVES

MELANY AND DUNCAN BERRY   LYNNE AND BILL TWIST   LILY YEH

LIFE MAPPING
for Your Authentic Journey ...185

Create your own action plan for sustaining personal health, and spiritual, emotional, and financial fulfillment. Explore your personal gifts and your passions, then create an individual map to highlight a pathway to balance, health, clarity, and joy.

Acknowledgments 201   **Resources** 204   **About the Full Bloomers** 210

About the Author 212   **Index** 214

Introduction

All around the world, a springtime of beauty and creativity is emerging from a long winter of dormancy. This new culture once again values the Earth, spirit, and compassion over the accumulation of possessions and the negativity that depletes the Earth and its soul. This shift in core values offers a more fulfilling and meaningful lifestyle to the individuals, couples, and families who are embracing their passions, living their dreams, and reweaving their communities with care and kindness. When social cooperation is scaled up, personal and global crises are transformed into opportunity. If we can get past anger, fear, pain, and poverty and allow old structures to decay, we inspire new and resilient systems to sprout and fruit in their place. Being mindful about the way we govern, what we teach, the food we eat, and the medical care we offer and receive means we can move toward social and environmental understanding and justice.

My Journey to Full Bloom

I have been on a lifelong journey of discovery and learning, touched by the beauty of Nature and the many altruistic individuals I've met in my travels. The book you hold in your hands is my offering to you—a bouquet of experiences and joy I've lovingly gathered and arranged—to inspire you to learn, engage, and contribute in whatever way you can. When you live your life in Full Bloom, it is like falling in love all over again. You are filled with delight and a sense of direction. Life is good. Life has meaning. Your creativity is juicier. You're in harmony with all of the world. Your awareness increases, your heart sings with gratitude, and you honor all living things. This is your invitation to bring more beauty, fun, and soulfulness into your life. It is my hope that you can awaken and cultivate compassion and direction for yourself, for your work, for Nature, and for your community. I want to inspire you to live life with your heart wide open.

I believe each of us has four distinct personality attributes—the Gardener, the Artist, the Lover, and the Spirit-Weaver—that create a framework for practicing mindfulness, unleashing potential, and revising a sense of play. As a Gardener, you observe, nurture, and grow. As an Artist, you use creativity to discover new possibilities. As a Lover, you lead with your heart and commit to things you're passionate about, and as

a Spirit-Weaver, you use celebrations and rituals to express blessings and gratitude. It may be that you're not currently exploring these facets of your life. Still, you can begin to immerse yourself in the small, but powerful practices I offer to build interpersonal connections, define the purpose of your busy life, figure out who you really are, and unearth your passions and gifts so you can go forth, bloom, and spread seeds of goodness all around.

I AM A GARDENER

I have loved Nature since childhood, and very early on I discovered gardens to be sanctuaries where I could form intimate relationships

with plants. The elderly ladies in my neighborhood caught me stealing their flowers, so they kindly invited me in and taught me how to garden. A woman named Ginger gave me my first Cecile Brunner climbing rose, and I planted it on my playhouse and grew my own baby pink roses for fairy crowns. At seventeen, I was an exchange student in a small village between Kyoto and Nara, Japan, where gardens were both sacred space—connecting my spirit to Nature—and works of art. Just a year later, I left my hometown in northern California to live off the land in Maine, learning organic gardening from my mentors, Scott and Helen Nearing. I went on to teach it in college, where I trained as a naturalist with Audubon and earned a degree in environmental studies, with a minor in art. I taught children and teens in residential programs about Nature, always weaving together gardening, creativity, and the natural world.

When I first visited Monet's gardens in Giverny, France, I fell completely and utterly in love. In 1985, I quit my job as a professional gardener with a crew of nine in Carmel, California, to work *for free* in France—spending the winter in Paris learning French and returning to Giverny in early spring, just as the gardens were coming out of dormancy. In the early mornings and late evenings, I photographed and wrote, day after day. I was following my own passions, and the path led me to a career as a professional photographer, artist, and writer. I return to Giverny every year to photograph the gardens for publications and exhibitions with Monet's paintings, and each time—just as when I visit the Amazon rain forest of Ecuador or spend time in the gardens of close friends—my intimacy with Nature deepens and expands. Nature is the teacher for my soul.

I AM AN ARTIST

In 1991, I decided to spend six months living very simply in a three hundred-year-old barn in a small village on the Normandy coast in France. It was a life-changing immersion: I had cold water, an outside toilet, and a camp stove—and no phone, TV, radio, or computer, but I was surrounded by great gardens, inspiring artists, and natural beauty. I followed the light. I photographed at dawn and dusk. I painted and wrote. And I had what I like to call "my coming-out party as an artist"—two major art shows in Pacific Grove and Hayward, California. The shows, named *Gardens Real and Imagined*, included my paintings, photography, interactive pieces, and altars. I vowed that art would no longer be a side job.

I listened to my deepest calling and recommitted to making my living in a multifaceted creative manner, including writing, photography, painting, garden design, teaching, lecturing, and more. I believe that riches can come in more forms than a paycheck—they come in flexibility of time, enjoyment of work, and fulfillment of soul. Since then, I've taught creativity to thousands of diverse people—from employees at Fortune 500 companies to indigenous youth in the Amazon rain forest to First Nations people in the wilderness of Haida Gwaii in northwestern British Columbia. It's an immense pleasure for me to help people lose their self-consciousness and just play; it's amazing what pours forth from each person and how surprising and delightful the outcome can be. Whether it's bringing back the arts to schools or engaging the senses and body with dance, music, or theater, I believe that creative expression leads to critical thinking, which, in turn, leads to innovative action.

I AM A LOVER

I used to be embarrassed when I'd get a lump in my throat from being so deeply touched by a child, by beauty, or by my beliefs. I constantly fall in love with people of all ages, with different places, and with animals, flowers, music, learning, and spirit. As I gained more self-acceptance, I realized that I needed to celebrate my heart connections instead of hiding them. The capacity of my heart has been expanded, like a field plowed open, by loving fully and by losing those I loved.

When my husband and soulmate, Gerald, was diagnosed with brain cancer, he went through a horrendous operation, had to relearn how to talk and walk, endured barbaric radiation treatments, and then died just eight months into our marriage. It felt like my heart had broken apart all the way to the bottom tip. During my time in deep mourning, I

wrote the book *Cultivating Sacred Space: Gardening for the Soul* as both a healing path and an offering. On a twelve-day vision quest in the desert with cultural anthropologist Angeles Arrien, I had a vivid image of Gerald's love pouring down, like liquid gold, into my heart—strengthening it with an enormous capacity for holding more love. I saw my heart begin to bloom with flowers in profuse abundance. I realize that it was like the Rumi poem—"Break my heart. Oh, break it again, so I can love more fully." My broken heart was able to love more fully. I made a commitment to live my life to the fullest, to remain always open and blooming, and to inspire others to live fully with love and creativity.

I AM A SPIRIT-WEAVER

My mom, an artist, spiritual seeker, and lover of Nature, became ill when I was about ten years old. She died on my twenty-first birthday, her body ravaged by cancer. To commemorate her life, I helped organize several different ceremonies and celebrations, representing all of her diversity. And I've been doing the same thing for friends and family for forty years: making rites for deaths, weddings, blessings, and passages. I feel it's a sacred act to arrange the flowers, lead the ceremonies, and weave together happiness, healing, and love for the special people in my life. I've studied and participated in many cross-cultural traditions around the world, and Spirit-Weaving has become a part of my personal practice. I bring God, the Mystery, and the Spirit into each day with thanks, with requests for guidance and with meditation. Though I've been called a medicine woman, I know that everyone has a healing medicine to offer, whether it's a song, a touch, or simply the way you comfort someone.

Finding Your Own Path

Each of us carries seeds of the Gardener, Artist, Lover, and Spirit-Weaver within, and with an awareness of these four pathways, you can rediscover, nurture, and bring into bloom a vision for your own life journey. The pathways in the first section of *Living Life in Full Bloom* represent what I hold most dear and what I wish to offer to you. I am deeply concerned about the well-being of our precious Earth, climate change, social justness, and spiritual connection. I developed these practices to bring more meaning with less materialism, more happiness with less despair, and more fulfillment with less longing. The Gardener pathway will lead you to a personal, more intimate relationship with Nature. The Artist pathway will expand your imagination and inspire creative expression in all parts of your life. The Lover pathway will invite you to open your heart in deeper ways and commit to what you love. The Spirit-Weaver pathway will bring celebrations, gratitude, and joy into each day.

In the second section, you'll meet the Full Bloomers, inspiring individuals and couples who exemplify a life of service and fulfillment and who are in partnership with their local communities and with international organizations focused on people, creativity, Nature, and teaching. You'll discover rich examples of how each person has incorporated each pathway into a thriving life, following their passions and infusing their work with love and meaningful contribution. Be inspired by remarkable individuals like Lily Yeh, who heals broken lives and brings peace and reconciliation through her stunning international community art projects, and Lynne and Bill Twist, founders of The Pachamama Alliance, which partners with indigenous people to save the rain forest—the lungs of the Earth. You won't forget Betty Peck, who has been bringing the garden to Kindergarten education for sixty years, and Lita Judge, delightful children's book author and illustrator who finds healing while creating her art. Meet Melany and Duncan Berry, whose entrepreneurial ventures consciously synthesize spiritual beliefs with environmental ethics, and David Baum and Terry Reeves, who weave community with magic, humor, and creativity at home and internationally. Each and every one of these Full Bloomers will inspire you to follow your passions and create a meaningful life of contribution and delight.

In the third section, you'll be invited to create your own Life Map, recognizing where you've been and where you may want to go. This step-by-step exercise helps you map your own journey, identifies your skills and passions, and helps you to gather tools and lessons from your pathway practices. You'll identify big and small community needs, both locally and far afield. The possibilities for personal growth and fulfillment are vast, and I am certain that with your Life Map in heart and hand, you will be inspired to take specific actions to serve the greater good.

We are at a turning point in time for the Earth and its people. I feel that we are being called to bring forward our gifts, to revive our communities with care and compassion, and to make sea changes to protect the health of the planet. By shifting from overconsumption to soulful contribution, we can find a better way to connect awareness with action and welcome a Full Bloom into a life of meaning and service—in a way that honors the Earth, the spirit, and one another with joy. Won't you join me?

Elizabeth Murray

Today, each of us is being called to connect, protect, and celebrate
all forms of Life on Earth—for our own meaning and purpose
and for the generations to come.

THE FOUR PATHWAYS

Explore each path to cultivate your soul and lead you to a life of greater meaning, purpose, and joy. You can start with *Gardener,* deepening your relationship with Nature. Proceed through *Artist* to expand your creativity and imagination. Onto *Lover,* where you'll open your heart and fall in love with life. Then complete your personal journey with *Spirit-Weaver* to integrate mindfulness, celebration, and blessings into each day. You are invited to explore these pathways at your own pace and in your own style. You may prefer to move around, beginning with the pathway that most calls you. You may work with some practices for a day; others may become a practice for life. Even when you do just one practice in each pathway, you'll find your life beginning to bloom. May you walk your path with curiosity, delight, and intention.

The path of the

Gardener

Deepening Your
Relationship with Nature

Following the path of the Gardener, you become more intimate with Nature and deepen your relationship with the Earth. Each day brings awe, wonder, and gratitude. Working with the soil, weather, and plants, you return to naturally slower rhythms. You nurture your life in tune with the living Earth, cultivating a beautiful and sustainable lifestyle. You collaborate with the elements to discover your personal ECOnomy. You learn from Nature's model that there is no waste; all is used and reused, and soil is as precious as gold. You welcome bees and pollinators and those creatures in the unseen world that so generously support life. You prune and weed what is no longer viable. You make compost to enrich the soil—deep, dark, and rich like your own soul. You become patient as you see how the passage of time brings results. Maturity is honored, and change is encouraged. You know the consequence of your actions or procrastination. You feel mysteriously prepared and supported as you reweave the web of life where connections have been broken. Your inner world of mindfulness supports your healthy body. Seeds of change are nurtured. From keen observation and just being, you experience the sacred in all things as you create your own sanctuary for renewal. Walking through the humble garden gate, you enter a portal to the divine natural world. Here you are deeply nurtured as you feel connected to all of creation. Awe and wonder return with the passing of each season. The everyday gifts of the sunrise, the beauty of flowers, warmth and light, and the vastness of stars teach you about gratitude for the common and the mysterious. You celebrate the blossoms and are grateful for the harvest. You find yourself in rhythm with Nature.

"No Mud, No Lotus."
—Thich Nhat Hanh

Ahh and Awe

A good way to be present in our bodies is to breathe mindfully, gently, and with compassion for others and ourselves.

I hold a handful of
seed,
**Feeling Life Force
Potential;**
I smile.

I put my hands in
soil,
**Feeling Life Force
Potential;**
I smile.

**I plant the seeds
with joy.
I water with love.
My garden
blooms;**
I smile.

My heart blooms,
Seeds of loving
kindness,
Blow in the wind;
We all smile.

The action of saying "Ahh" as a full, deep expelling of the breath—accompanied purposefully by the sound "Ahh"—can make it easier to fully relax and come home to ourselves. Breathing "Ahh" can be our meditation and a means of letting go of tensions that we may be holding deep within ourselves and of daily concerns that make our shoulders go up around our ears. These stresses can be a long-standing ache, a disturbing thought, or a nagging worry. But with "Ahh," we can be our own loving mother, saying to ourselves, "Ahh, there you are, dear one. I see you. I recognize you. I will comfort you, love you, and accept you."

Awe is to enter a childlike state of wonder and delight. It happens when we are able to let go of the adult complications that surround us day to day and to permit ourselves to see the miracles of everyday life with a child's innocent appreciation. Then we are able to find the extraordinary in the ordinary, the magical in the mundane. In awe, we draw in our breath, inhaling deeply in admiration of that which enchants us.

PRACTICE: As you walk barefoot in your garden or in any natural place, step slowly and plant the soles of your feet firmly on Mother Earth. Inhale the serenity of the garden and gently awaken your sense of awe. Then exhale slowly with an "Ahh." Breathe out your stress and worry. Look with innocent eyes at the wonder that surrounds you. Notice the garden's fresh new growth. Identify the sensation that awakens your inner awe or presents you with a comforting "Ahh" moment.

Finding Wildness Within

Entering your garden, you're invited to know it as the wild place it actually is.

No matter what stage the garden is in—from the first bed outlined to a full-blown, floral-filled landscape—its original wild nature still exists.

All gardens have soil brimming with the unseen world of beneficial microbes, fungi, and worms—and even, perhaps, as in my garden, unwelcome gophers or moles. You might have visiting deer that can eat up your prized begonias overnight, or they might be welcome guests because they add graceful beauty in a woodland or native garden. I invite wildness into my garden. Long ago, I removed all the lawns and replaced them with meadows and wildflowers. Gophers and wind have edited ground and trees far more severely than I ever would have done; I am not in control, and the wildness expresses itself in its own spontaneous ways.

Having elements of wildness presents an opportunity to rediscover your inner wild nature. Being in touch with your own wildness allows you to be free of comparisons and jealousies, and brings you back to the authentic nature you had before you were molded into what your parents or society desired. From this place, you can access your spirit, creativity, and the uncensored parts of your original voice.

PRACTICE: Embrace the untamed parts of yourself and allow part of your garden to return to its wildness. Scatter wildflower seeds, grow native plants, or plant a meadow instead of a tidy green lawn. Allow vegetable vines to wither after the harvest and collect the seeds, and appreciate the beauty of wildness and the wildlife that comes to dine. Then, find wildness in yourself, too. Go outside in the rain, bask on a rock, climb a tree, lie on the grass, dance with abandon, and be wild with Nature.

Create Sacred Space

Creating sacred space in our gardens makes a profound statement of intention—a proclamation about our connection to the world around us and how we live within it.

The garden has always been my personal sanctuary—a place for my soul to be nurtured, to grow, and to blossom.

Being present in our actions and mindful that all of Nature is directly connected to spirituality, in whatever form that may take. Anything done with love is really a sacred act.

Garden altars provide an opportunity to express personal spirituality with or without reflecting specific doctrines. I have always made different kinds of altars in my garden and home, each one created with a different purpose or intent: as a focal point for a ceremony, as a place to meditate, or as an axis mundi, the earthly center that connects us to the realms of the spirit above, below, and all around us. In Japan, people stop at street shrines to offer prayers as they go about their busy days. In Bali, home gardens usually have at least seven shrines, with each placed in one of the sacred directions.

Typically, altars are created as platforms, tables, or raised mounds and are the focal point in ceremonies, rituals, and celebrations. On the altar, you can place offerings of flowers or fruits from the garden; light candles, symbolizing the light you bring to the world; and burn incense, allowing its smoke to carry your wishes, prayers, and intentions upward. Temples, churches, and synagogues around the world use flowers as decoration for their sacred spaces.

PRACTICE: **To create sacred space in your garden, identify an area that speaks most clearly to your soul. Is it under a specific tree or a corner of quietude that whispers its attraction to you with the flutter of a bird's wings? Your own personal altar in the garden can be made by adding a meaningful statue perhaps of an angel, Buddha, the Virgin Mary, St. Francis, or even St. Fiacre, the patron saint of gardeners. A large stone or bench can invite contemplation. Take time each day to sit in your sacred space and let it become the focus for meditation and prayer, as well as a spot to pay tribute to ancestors or beloved pets.**

Welcoming the Birds

Once you create a garden, no matter what the size, the first visitors will be wild birds.

They peck across the newly dug flowerbeds like party guests around a buffet. Mourning doves come in pairs, and wrens dart out from beneath a leaf. The garden comes alive with their chatter.

There are many ways to put out the welcome mat. Birdbaths, birdhouses, and bird feeders all offer hospitality, as does planting specific berries for food and having shrubs and trees for habitat and nesting. Birding is a captivating hobby that enriches our lives at any age. You will soon become familiar with—and delighted by—the huge variety of creatures that will come to visit, as they know the space you've created is a friendly one.

In our own gardens, the simple act of replenishing a bird feeder is a personal offering to Nature. I love giving bird feeders to elderly people and children. They invariably share the news of their visiting birds. It is a joyous way to encourage children's ability to observe. What do the birds look like? What are their special behaviors?

When Teddy Roosevelt was a child, he had poor eyesight but he could imitate hundreds of birdcalls and did so even when he was president. His love of birds led him first to a love of Nature, then to his friendship with John Muir, and ultimately to the creation of the national park system, which has since saved many spectacular natural features across the land. Cross-culturally, birds have long been regarded as symbols of departed souls and messengers from heaven, and are thought to carry the secrets to enlightenment. Many individual bird species hold rich mythology and meaning.

> Birdsong opens my wild heart.
> Curious I search the garden.
> Who brings this joy
> of color and song?
> Teach my wild heart
> to praise.

PRACTICE: Invite more birds into your garden by putting up a feeder, adding a birdbath, or offering a birdhouse. Spend an hour outdoors as often as you can to watch the birds fly and listen to them sing. Imagine yourself in free flight above the treetops, looking down on the beautiful and challenged Earth, and consider how you might bring more wisdom and peace to your world. Birds thrive equally in the world of Earth and sky—what insights might you carry with you, soaring between heaven and Earth?

Breathe

Breathing as a relaxation technique is an ancient practice and can be used at any time to increase your vitality and happiness.

PRACTICE: Head outside to a garden terrace, porch, park, or wild area. Sit directly on the ground or lean against a tree with your bare feet planted firmly on the Earth. Take even breaths, in and out. Enjoy your breath and be aware of the pleasure of being in Nature. As you breathe, consider how you share the same air with the weather, the coolness or warmth, the breeze, and the sun. Which scents does the air carry? Can you smell the current season? Can you feel the season with your cheeks? Can you hear the season? As you breathe, bring an awareness of the garden into your body. Slow down your thoughts, inhale with a mindful focus, and feel the union of your body with the natural world.

Your breath is always available to you—to quiet your mind, to be present in your body, and to become one with your environment. A breath of fresh air can cultivate your inner garden and bring a joyful awareness to the moment.

When working in the garden, take short breaks to breathe in deeply and feel gratitude for Nature as you exhale. Maybe you hear a tree rustling its autumn leaves (thank you for the miracle of life), see bees buzzing busily as they harvest pollen (thank you for abundant food), or feel drops of gentle spring showers (thank you for rainfall). When you are driving, walking, or rushing around, remember to breathe in and know that you are taking in the wind of inspiration. Exhale toward your goal and know that another inspiring breath is there for you to take and lead you forward through your day.

Breathe in your garden
Breathe out your joy
Your body breathes in the garden
Your garden breathes in your body
Garden and body are one
You are home
Happiness.

Butterflies, Transformation, and You

Butterflies have long represented spirituality and immortality, and they are potent symbols of transformation and the soul.

They begin their life cycle as caterpillars, creeping slowly along leaf edges and branches. At this stage, they are voracious eaters, consuming nourishment equal to hundreds of times their body weight and fortifying themselves for the next stage in their maturity: the chrysalis. Cocooned in a self-spun silken pod, they enter a mummy-like dormancy, during which all of their cells liquefy into imaginal cells and completely manifest into a new life-form: the elegantly sculpted, angel-winged creatures that flit above our gardens. We're witnesses to one of Nature's great evolutionary miracles.

Humans, too, have the ability to metamorphose—to grow from babies to teenagers, from teenagers to adults. As a culture, we are being invited to transform ourselves from a nation of avaricious consumers to a community of sensitive citizens who aim to live lightly on the Earth. We are invited to reimagine our lives and stop devouring ever more of Earth's dwindling resources, and instead reach within ourselves to enrich and sustain our lives, just like the graceful butterfly.

Butterfly species are facing extinction as native habitat is erased by development, pollution, and other man-made intrusions. I encourage you to create a sanctuary of native plants, shrubs, and trees that offers caterpillars a place to build a cocoon and offers butterflies the nectar of life. In return, butterflies will be like flying flowers, and their gentle movement will pollinate your garden, inspiring you to move forward softly but surely, as well.

PRACTICE: Learn about butterflies in your area and welcome them to your garden by including the best host plants for larvae and adults. Where I live, we are blessed with the sights and stopovers of migrating monarchs, so it's imperative that I plant milkweed for the larvae to eat and offer a shallow bowl of water so the butterflies can continue on their life's journey. Your soul seeks connection with Nature and beauty, so imagine butterflies as your personal teacher. Consider what you need to feed your own transformation. What will motivate you to emerge from your chrysalis and spread your wings? What part of you will metamorphose into a new beautiful form? What—and who—will support your process of growth and change?

Invite a Child into the Garden

My friend Betty Peck believes that every child should have a sandbox with a water source so they can re-create the rivers of the world and learn how mountains, valleys, and hills are formed.

As a teacher, Betty gave her Kindergarteners one small wooden barrel of rainwater a day so they could see how much water they were using, and she taught them that water is a precious resource, only replenishing itself through raindrops. The value and wonder of water is a lesson for all of us to practice.

It is natural for children to play, imagine, and invent, but adults have a much harder time inviting their inner child out to play. It is so delightful to get entirely dirty while scooping, shaping, and squishing mud between your toes. My friend Margot encourages children to make "mud kisses" by shaping sticky mud into little pyramids and pressing in flower seeds. The kisses are left to bake in the sun, and when they're dry, the children give the kisses to family and friends to grow in their gardens. Kids grow, seeds grow, love grows!

Think back to your favorite outdoor spot when you were a child. Was it a sandbox, the wide-open garden, or a tree with a branch at the perfect height to climb? When I was a child, one of my favorite places was a tree house we built ourselves, a place of our very own, where we could be alone and discover the heart of a tree and Nature from our own perspective.

PRACTICE: Invite a child (or the child within your soul) to explore the magic, hidden, and unseen world of your garden. Make magic potions from plants and dolls from flowers. Can you find a secret spot between hedges? Make a fairy house with miniature furniture or collect pebbles for a mosaic. Get creative! Turn on a sprinkler and run through it. Make a wish with a dandelion. Jump in a pile of leaves. Experience the garden with a child for more joy!

Create a Fairy Mailbox

As a child, I knew all about the leprechauns who lived under our apple tree and the fairies and elves who lived in the garden.

Perhaps you built little fairy houses of sticks and moss or had a secret place where the fairies could leave messages if they felt you had done something special. Growing up can be magical, especially if you're surrounded by the awe-inspiring wonder of the natural world. Telling stories about flower fairies, elves, and other Nature spirits strengthens children's connection to the unseen worlds, Nature, and their own imagination.

You might discover you have a natural fairy mailbox in a crag of a tree or an old stump, or you could create one. Children will be amazingly helpful at finding the perfect spot for such a mail drop. My first mailbox was by the sidewalk in an old tree with a heart-shaped hole in its age-gnarled trunk. I encouraged my niece and neighbor children to write notes to the fairies, and leave the notes and gifts of flowers in the tree trunk. At night, the fairies would remove the notes and would often write tiny messages in green ink back to the children on scraps of paper. Each little scroll was tied with a golden thread. Fairies would answer questions such as: Are fairy wings like butterfly wings? Do fairies ever ride on butterflies or hummingbirds?

I had the honor of being a fairy scribe and would help answer questions at times when there was more correspondence than the fairies could keep up with on their own! This kind of immersion into a garden and the imagination of the child will delight both of you and establish a shared personal connection to Nature that will endure for life.

PRACTICE: Discover or create a fairy mailbox in your garden or near a local school, library, or park, and encourage the children in your life to write notes to the fairies. Leave your own notes! You will be surprised how quickly you will become the fairy scribe and how your own imagination and playfulness will be vividly ignited along with that of the child's.

The Beauty of a Bloom

Flowers are an essential part of Nature as well as an important part of every culture on Earth.

PRACTICE: Take time to really see and admire a flower and all of its intricate parts. Grow flowers in your garden that represent the things you love. Select blossom colors that make you feel happy and fragrant flowers to enrich your senses like aromatherapy. Flowers can be a metaphor for life—they bud, open fully, and eventually drop their petals for fruit and seed. Each day offers a new opportunity for blossoming.

Brought from the wild and cultivated for their beauty, they are used to enhance social activities and celebrations, to decorate, and to provide food, medicine, comfort, and scent.

I've found that flowers can communicate. One busy day, I had my kitchen open to the garden. Two bright pink Shirley poppies in the window box outside the door had begun to reach inside the doorway. As I walked in and out, I would say to them, "You are so beautiful." Suddenly I realized the flowers wanted me to stop and really look at them. So I did, and then I realized that they wanted me to photograph them. I stopped everything and got out my camera and close-up lens. And when I really began to see them, I was drawn into a sort of healing vortex and into another world. I was stunned. These photographs have since become healing mandalas. Looking at them helps increase my mental clarity and relieve stress.

Some years ago, the organizers of a new garden show in Tokyo asked me to design a logo. As I was walking to the beach, a pink rock rose seemed to whisper, "I am the logo." I looked at it and realized, "Yes, of course, you are it!" This flower has five heart-shaped petals, and at the base of each petal is a triangle that becomes part of a five-pointed star with a golden center.

I believe that flowers are here to share beauty and to open hearts, so I feel it is important to admire them with gratitude. I have noticed, too, that photographing a flower is like photographing a woman: For best results, ask permission first, admire the flower's beauty, and then say thank you.

"If we could see the miracle of a single flower clearly, our whole life would change." —Buddha

Greet the Dawn

Choose a day to awaken before dawn and be ready to greet the day's first light.

Dress warmly and go out to watch the sky wake up as the sun rises and the moon recedes. You might be fortunate enough to see the very last glimmer of the stars while the moon hangs still in the waning horizon. Listen for the first birdsong, the first individual chirp that wakes the dawn chorus, as the early birds announce themselves and prepare to conduct the symphony of new light that is on its way.

Notice the time of year, the day's weather, where you are in the world, and how the beginning of a new day makes you feel. Fill your senses with this magic moment of the great turning, when your corner of the Earth turns once again toward the sun and the night sky recedes. Your experience is totally unique yet universal as well. Feel it; breathe it in.

How often have we missed this magic dawn in exchange for sleepy, cozy warmth? When I give myself the gift of rising before the sun, I know I am a part of an ancient rite of welcoming and anticipation. In the deep jungle of southern Ecuador, I have shared my dreams with the Achuar people. Their culture values the individual's dreams, and at dawn each day, they gather to share dreams. An elder interprets each dream to inform the person's day according to the meaning and direction of the dream.

PRACTICE: Rise before dawn. Light a candle to guide your way outside or to a large window. Admire the soft colors as they appear on the horizon. Let the dawn light inspire you. Appreciate this new day as a gift like no other. Choose to embrace it with intention and mindfulness. What would you like to dedicate this day to—a loved one, an action you want to take, or an opportunity to express peace, love, courage, clarity? Gather your dreams and consider what they say about your aspirations for your inner personal garden and the garden you share with the world.

"We must learn to reawaken and keep ourselves awake, not by mechanical aids, but by an infinite expectation of the dawn."
—Henry David Thoreau

Savor Food with Gratitude

Blessings on the meal!

PRACTICE: Buy your food from local organic growers and producers, and strive to grow food in your own garden. Invite friends over to cook. Search out new and different recipes—ethnic foods connect us to the people of the world and the global dining table! Eat entirely vegetarian meals at least once a week for health of body and Earth. And before you eat, express gratitude for the food by blessing the growers, the elements, and the cooks. I like to hold hands with my guests and bless our meal together. Conscious food consumption—eating with purpose and gratitude—helps to develop new, more healthful eating patterns and to increase the appreciation you have for the abundance in your life.

When you put your hands in the Earth and tend seeds, you are cultivating paradise. If you grow some of the vegetables you eat in a biodiverse garden with fruit trees and culinary herbs, you bring sensual abundance into the world each day. Nourish yourself and your family with delicious food from your garden and the local farmers' market. Nutritious fresh food brings health and vitality to your life, spirit, and emotion. Every meal invites a conscious practice to connect to the Earth with blessings and gratitude. Meals can be a daily act of love, nurturing everyone at the table.

I love making huge pots of soup with ingredients I find in season at the local farmers' market. I offer soup as a gift for comfort or celebration, and I preserve the harvest by putting up quarts of soup in the freezer for the days when I don't have time to cook. Knowing that there's soup for another day gives me a sense of wealth and abundance. I am also thankful for the times I can share the kitchen and cook with friends, with music, wine, and conversation as the central part of our evening social time together.

When we honor Nature and the web of life, show respect for diversity, support pollinators in the garden, feed our soils, and practice right and conscious use of water resources, we become part of a sustainable lifestyle that is better for everyone and our living Earth. And that's something we can all be grateful for.

"The grateful heart sits at a continuous feast."

—Proverbs 15:15

Purposeful Happiness

His Holiness the Dalai Lama teaches that the purpose of life is happiness.

When we lead our lives with the aim of becoming truly happy, everything shifts. You can feel and express gratitude and joy, even if everything isn't perfect.

As a Gardener, what would make you truly happy? What would your garden be like? Would you grow delicious vegetables all year and have a lovely orchard of fruit? Would you have a pond with water lilies and fish? Would your place of delight be a formal knot garden or a wild meadow? Would your garden invite children to play with a tree house and a rope swing? Would you have so many flowers that you could pick bouquets for your house and to give away and still have plenty in the garden? Do you appreciate the wild abandon of a self-seeded flower, an overgrown vine, and a bursting perennial bed?

I am very happy visiting different styles of gardens, yet I know my own garden must be in balance with its natural resources and self-sufficient because of the limited resources of water and my time to tend it. Wildness, diversity, and a feeling of the seasons make me

happy. I love to discover natural surprises, and I accept imperfection. One rose can make me happy—"Oh good! Welcome. No one ate you!" Your garden and the activity of gardening brings great pleasure and joy to you and to others—contentment and satisfaction rolled into one. By creating a garden and working in it yourself, you'll find a purposeful happiness just being in the space you've created.

PRACTICE: Reflect on what will truly bring you happiness and set your priorities to that. Release perfection and comparison to others, and give yourself the opportunity to relax, soften your gaze, and appreciate your space and who you are. Make a path to happiness through your garden, be curious and full of wonder over the life-and-death rhythms of the seasons and natural change. Study and absorb the beauty of the light, the sparkle of dew, and the innocent grace of a newly opened flower—they last just a moment. Take time to smile so that your heart will bloom, too. The commitment to release control and embrace change and happiness in your garden can transform your life and can inspire a new way of living.

The Allure of Herbs

Herbs—one of the most intriguing, diverse, and useful plant groups—are as rich in myth and meaning as they are in scent, texture, flavor, and color.

PRACTICE: Plant a few culinary herbs to use in cooking. Choose one herb to research, plant, and tend for a year. Notice how you feel smelling it and being near it. See if you can learn something directly from the plant itself. Or research its literary connotations. This could be the beginning of a diverse new plant relationship and way to interact with the plant world, as well as a way to connect with poets, visionaries, apothecaries, and culinary traditions that stretch back across the millennia.

Herbs are both modest and profound. The old-fashioned name for herbs was "simples."

Culinary herb gardens are best planted close to the kitchen door so their leaves, seeds, bulbs, and blossoms are at hand to flavor food when needed. A physic garden is made up of medicinal herbs to use as remedies for a multitude of ailments, from headaches to heartbreaks.

Many people who know plant medicine suggest choosing just one plant to get to know intimately over a year. Blue-flowered rosemary is a good one to begin with because it has many uses. It has a rich lore and brings great charm to the garden border or a container garden. I use it for soups, with roast potatoes and chicken, and blended with salt and pepper as a rub. For healing, rosemary can relieve congestion or be used as a facial—put a few fresh twigs in boiling water to release the natural oils, and then breathe the steam or let it soothe the pores of your skin. Shakespeare had Ophelia say, "There's rosemary, that's for remembrance," and traditionally a whiff of rosemary from a sprig of the herb carried in a pocket helped to stimulate memory. I have given it to children who are taking tests, and I brought it to the hospital for my husband to smell after his brain surgery to help him regain his memory. I know the earthy pungent scent reminded him of our garden, far away from the confines of the sterile hospital room.

"There's rosemary, that's for remembrance.
Pray, love, remember." —Hamlet

Coming Home

The word *home* used to make me cry; I longed for it so deeply.

I yearned for my own bit of Earth and a sense of belonging to place. I have made gardens since childhood, but there was a period of time when I lived in twenty places in less than ten years. I carried my potted plants with me or gave them away.

Many of us feel a sense of being unrooted. Moving around is common today; the average stay in one place is just three years—so different from fifty years ago when we stayed in family homes for decades. This affects how we form commitments to our community, work with each other, and shape our values. We live in disposable times. Yet gardening can be the path that connects you to land and natural life cycles, bringing meaning and purpose into your life and allowing you to experience a sense of belonging. When you've found that place of "home," you'll find that hope and optimism bloom. As a Gardener, you will become a keeper of land and you'll realize that the land keeps you as well. This reciprocal relationship allows the natural and human world to mutually thrive.

When I plant seeds and then care for my plants, their growth, beauty, and food enrich me. By knowing a garden well, you form a relationship with commitment and familiarity. This is home, essential for re-rooting to place and your own thriving. What you learn in the garden—awareness of weather, soil, water, health, and the importance of thriving ecosystems—you bring to all parts of your life. You can connect to all things with gratitude.

PRACTICE: Look around at the garden you've created, inherited, or visit. Whether it is new or old, consider what feels most familiar. Was that rose from your mother's garden? Did a friend give you those flowerpots? Did you discover beautiful bulbs that bloom in spring? All of the things in a garden speak to a life rich with people, experience, joy, woe, success, and failure. Imagine yourself being rooted—in your heart, belly, and inner self—like a tree to this place and this piece of ground. Feel at home.

"There's a magical tie to the land of our home, which the heart cannot break, though the footsteps may roam." —Eliza Cook

One Step at a Time

Every life follows a path, one step at a time. Metaphorically, paths represent our life purpose, our process, and our pace.

✿ PRACTICE: Find a variety of paths to walk, whether they're in your garden, at the park, through the woods, or in a neighborhood. Walk in silence, one step at a time, opening your senses and awareness. Be present and in appreciation. Your walking meditation will stimulate the visionary within.

There is no path to happiness: happiness is the path.

—Buddha

The materials we choose to create a path—as well as the route it takes, the patterns it employs, and the elements alongside it—all contribute to its meaning and your pace.

Garden paths, permanent or informal, connect us to different places. Spiral paths allow you to move inward to enrich your soul. Labyrinths have been used for thousands of years in diverse cultures around the world and symbolize descent into the unknown and resurrection with new insight, as if you're entering the womb of Mother Earth. Labyrinths echo your inner path—there are no dead ends, you can never get lost, and you always walk the right path.

Meandering paths welcome you to walk and meditate for inner guidance. Often laid out with stepping-stones to slow your pace, these paths connect you to your senses and activate your creative spirit.

A straight path may be designed as an axis in a garden. In meditation, the axis of consciousness is a path from the head to the heart. Our challenge is to remove the obstacles or distractions. It is the spine, connecting thought with action and heart with mind. Monet's garden in France has a central axis—the Grande Allée connects his house to the foot of the Japanese bridge in the water garden across the road. It is the main feature of the garden, with arches covered in climbing roses that connect a pair of raised perennial beds. This flourishing tunnel is carpeted with creeping nasturtiums, transforming a straight, broad walk into a blooming tunnel with a meandering pathway for eye and foot. Where does your path lead you?

Learn from Permaculture

Permaculture promotes sustainability and self-reliance by creating diverse ecosystems for balance, beauty, and bounty—whether it's large-scale agriculture or your own backyard.

And it's an inspiring way to live, using Nature as your model and your mentor. The way you cook, solve problems, and even invest your money can be inspired by the proverbial lessons we're taught in Nature.

Appreciate "slow": Avoid instant landscapes created by planting plants too big for their space or fertilizing for fast growth.

Know your place: Notice how the sun moves across the garden, where it's sunny, and how the shade keeps areas cool.

Pay attention: What's the forecast, the direction of the wind, or the expected harvest?

Learn about runoff: How can you harness the rain? (I've made a rain garden to soak up downpours and collected as much as ten thousand gallons of water for my garden. Check your local codes.)

Diversify: Try removing your monoculture lawn and replanting it with a wild meadow or a vegetable garden.

Rotate: Vary what you plant and grow green cover crops like fava beans or red clover to replenish the soil. Plant fruit trees and flowers mixed with vegetables.

Integrate: Create multiple uses for each space. Even a small outdoor area can allow for dining, drying clothes, play, and even an outdoor shower.

Pay attention to the edges: That's where the magic is! If you're familiar with fairy realms, you know that the fringes hold immense riches.

Design with intention: Careful, thoughtful study of place combined with true purpose and goals will guarantee success.

PRACTICE: Observe the plants in your garden and how they interact. What are they telling you—too dry, not enough sun, drainage issues, or thriving? A plant's physical state reveals much about its happiness in a certain spot. Then, pay attention to where *you* are happiest. Stop, rest, explore, and enjoy your garden so it has time to teach you about your own sustainability and balance.

Play Like a Child

Lila is a Sanskrit word meaning "divine play," and it encompasses creation, destruction, re-creation, and love.

PRACTICE: **Find ways to play in your garden so you can lose yourself without attachment to outcome. If you can, invite a child to join you. Create art with flower petals, whistle using plant leaves, catch lightning bugs at night, make a sculpture with bamboo poles or long sticks tied together, or swing as high as you can. Forget your adulthood from time to time, and bring play into your garden—and into the other corners of your life.**

Essentially, that's what a garden is. And when you're engaged in having fun, it's timeless. Play, at all ages, sparks creativity and encourages risk taking, helping us to accept—even welcome—spontaneity and change. It stimulates curiosity, reminding us that life is about process and growth.

When children play in your garden, you can experience with them the sacredness of the space. How fun it is to smell the aromatic leaves and flowers, to taste herbs or edible flowers, to rub the fuzzy lamb's ear on our cheeks, listen to birdsong and wind chimes, and make fairy houses and habitats!

I have a rope swing in a grand American chestnut tree in my own garden, and not only does it draw children of all ages, but it also acts as a moving meditation for adults. You can glide into the branches and lush canopy of the tree, and, as you lean back, you can see the world from a new perspective—all filtered through the green lungs of its leaves. For children, climbing trees and finding a place to hide bring strength and a sense of adventure. Finding a comfortable branch to sit on puts children in charge of their world. My friend has a tire swing—a "ring of courage"—that swings down from a high perch in a treehouse. The ride makes you scream for the sheer joy of it! And it's a good life lesson: You only get the thrill if you're willing to take the risk.

Pollination: The Kiss of Life

Nothing—including humans—survives in Nature if it's fiercely independent or fiercely dependent.

We're designed to rely on one another and on all of Nature. We're all connected. Take pollination: There exists an intricate dance of a flower's beauty and its capacity to attract and invite an insect, a hummingbird, or a bat to visit and pollinate the flower so it can set fruit and make seed. The flower offers its sweet nectar in exchange for pollination.

I once captured a swarm of honeybees fifty feet off the ground. I was precariously balancing on a fire department ladder and leaning into a deodar cedar tree in our garden. While I hung high in the air, I cut off the branch where the swarm was attached, holding the buzzing ten-pound mass of life with one hand as I climbed down the ladder. My brother and I carefully tucked the swarm back into a new hive box, gently speaking to them to keep them calm. Each second of the process was a meditation of presence and life force, both exhilarating and frightening.

We would not have plants or food or our good health if it weren't for the pollinators. I've designed my garden with butterflies, bees, hummingbirds, and other pollinators in mind, knowing how important they are to the well-being of our planet. In the desert Southwest, bats play a role in the pollination of agave and saguaro; and in the tropics, many of our favorite fruits—mangoes, bananas, and guavas—depend on bats for pollination.

PRACTICE: Plant flowers for bees, butterflies, and hummingbirds, consulting your county extension office or pollinator.org for advice on native plants that attract pollinators. You can also participate in a bee cooperative, where apiarists tend the hives and you support their work by purchasing shares of the honey production. Or, if you have a real interest in bees and honey, consider a class and instruction in beekeeping. Watch the film *The Hidden Beauty of Pollination* by Louie Schwartzberg on YouTube.

Plant Seeds

Being a Gardener is both a literal and metaphoric way of living.

PRACTICE: **Before planting seeds, hold them in your hands, close your eyes, and feel their life potential. Think about the magic of each seed and how it will grow into a unique plant. Blow on them with your intention so they will flourish with your energy. Some people put organic vegetable seeds in their mouth to coat them with their DNA so they'll have a connection as they grow. Ask yourself: What other seeds of intention and desire do you tend in your life?**

> "To see things in the seed, that is genius."
>
> —Lao Tzu

It invites you to nurture, whether seed or self, and allows you to see the results of your labors and the blooming of your intentions. And the best way to become a gardener is to begin with the simple and profound act of planting seeds. No matter your skills or your apprehension in growing, planting seeds is where you'll find true magic.

If you're a beginner, start with loose-leaf lettuce and radish seeds. They're both easy and fast, and you'll be eating your own salad in twenty-eight days. Try planting some cheerful nasturtiums in a window box to enjoy in a salad—the flowers are both colorful and peppery! Nasturtium seed is big and easy to push into the soil one by one, at the edges of containers or the garden bed. I remember planting hundreds of these seeds in May down the entire length of Monet's Grande Allée, on both sides of the raised beds, and they were in full bloom and ready for the kitchen by late summer.

Attentiveness and Patience

Like all knowledge or spiritual practice, what you learn must sink in and not just remain on the surface in order to grow.

You've planted your lettuce seeds with intention, and they're on their own, germinating, with nothing more for you to do. Or is there? Now's the time when you get to be attentive, standing by and observing. Make sure the seedlings are getting enough sunlight—too little and they will emerge thin and wan. Check the moisture of the soil as the days go by and mist lightly with water to penetrate the Earth below the surface (not too strong of a water flow or it will disturb the seed).

Remember that seeds will take some days to germinate, so practice patience and faith. Trust that the seed coat has cracked open as it swells with moisture and that there are new signs of life below the surface of the soil. Soon, tiny roots will emerge, and then leaves will poke up, looking like a pair of green hearts. This is a very tender and magical time for plants, and they need your protection. Be sure that the soil stays evenly moist, and, if necessary, protect the tender shoots so they are not eaten by birds. Watch that the light is not too hot (they will burn) or too spare (they will be spindly and stretched).

I've learned from the Achuar women in the Amazon that it's helpful to sing to your garden plants while tending them. The songs connect with the spirit of the plants to form relationships—and then the plants thrive. Though there are many theories about music and plant growth and plant reactions to kind speech or negative words, I've found that any melody or kind words—delivered with loving intention—makes all life thrive.

PRACTICE: Seeds sown in the garden need your care to germinate and grow strong and vigorous. Your patience is needed as you watch and water and wonder! Sing a song to your plants to boost their growth. Seeds sown in your circle of love need kindness and care, too. Be especially mindful of the seeds of loving kindness you plant with friends and family, and be sure that you are nurtured daily.

Awaken Your Senses

Our senses play an important role in our lives, helping us to appreciate what we have and to discover new things.

PRACTICE: **Go out to the garden and awaken your senses. Breathe deeply and smell the season, the weather, or a freshly mowed lawn. Take a sprig of rosemary or dill and let it rest on your tongue. Look into the branches of a tree to see bark patterns, insect life, or a bird's nest. Listen for sounds of moving water or wind—or simply welcome the soft silence. Brush against leaves to feel their glossiness, their resin, and their jagged edges. Add plants to your garden that will enhance your sensual experience and increase your awareness of the ever-changing world.**

Our senses are a portal to the magic and imagination of the universe and every moment on Earth!

Being out in the garden stirs all your senses, awakens your soul, and allows you to feel present in the moment.

When you put your hands into soil or touch the soft, velvety leaves of lamb's ear, you are in *touch* with the living Earth—and the endorphins you release will make you feel happy. When you *see* sunlight streaming through a backlit leaf, it is the alchemical emblem of Khidr, the ancient Islamic "Verdant One" or "the Green One" who changes light into life. When you *hear* birdsong, you become more familiar with the habitat that supports the birds and the multitude of pitches and calls in the chorus of resident birds. When you eat fruit or vegetables that you've grown, you *taste* vitality, juiciness, and life itself. When you *smell* the aroma of honeysuckle and lavender, it can revive a powerful olfactory memory from another time, like the smell of a rose from your grandmother's garden.

As you take in the sun-warmed scent of the soil in which your fruit grows, you're partaking in a communion offered by the garden—a gift consisting of all the sensory elements, a bit of magic, and your own blessings from Nature. Your senses allow you to make a joyful connection to all the living creatures and plants in the garden.

The Soil and the Soul

Because soil is the Earth's mantle and supports all life, its health is directly connected to the health and well-being of every one of us.

And we can play an active role in enriching soil by composting.

Trust me, compost is gardener's gold. Begin with a "brown" layer of dried leaves and twigs, and heap on "green" organic waste from your kitchen and weeds from the garden (along with a bit of well-rotted manure, if it's available to you) to heat up the mix and help break it down. Some piles get hot enough to kill off any weed seeds; others are cooler and take longer to decompose. Leave it to sit, occasionally turning the pile over and adding water to keep it evenly moist. After a few weeks, a dark and rich humus develops. Add this magic mixture to your garden to add nutrients, improve moisture retention, promote good drainage, and support optimum plant health. Ultimately, the deeper, darker, and more fertile the soil is, the more certain it is to promote and sustain growth.

I find that soil and soul are strongly related to each other. When we delve into the rich darkness of our inner selves, weed out what is no longer serving us, and amend our lives with goodness, we emerge stronger and more confident, ready for vital growth and contribution through a process that feels as natural as the changing of the seasons.

> "The land often gives to us freely, asking much less in return than we get from it. So it is possible to see much more kindness in the world if we think beyond the human community and include the land in our thoughts, too."
>
> —Bob Rodale

PRACTICE: Keep your sense of humor as you identify areas in need of "compost" in your life. What needs enriching? What's ready for the decomposition process? What needs pruning to promote more light and stimulate growth? Build your emotional compost pile, and let it sit awhile to transform into something that will enrich your soul, your health, and your resilience so that you can bear productive fruit. Jot down your insights and your commitments on paper, and add them to your real compost pile. By the end of the season, your goals will be connected to the soil and can help you build a healthy personal ecosystem.

Eyes to the Sky

All of life is dependent on sunlight to grow, and as Gardeners we learn the specific light requirements of our plants so they can thrive.

PRACTICE: Really pay attention every time you go outside, day or night. The skies help us connect to our place in the universe. Take a moment to observe the sunlight and the way it moves across the sky, shines through misty morning fog, and creates ripples on the hottest days. Notice the wind and the rainfall, and how each changes throughout the garden and the year. Educate yourself—and the children in your life—about clouds and what each type of cloud tells you about the sky and weather conditions. When the conditions are particularly idyllic and beautiful, say thank you and allow yourself to feel a full connection to all of Nature. And check out the amazing app LivingEarth.

Beauty is always a part of the garden, and we can find joy in the way light enters and affects our garden: the sparkle of dewdrops in the apricot light of morning, the backlit leaves in early afternoon, and the glow of an orange sky at dusk. Light is a direct reminder of the sacred spirit around us. Sometimes it feels like grace to me. Inspired by Monet and other great painters and photographers, I have spent hours each day following the light, trying to catch moments on film or canvas.

Clear blue skies are especially lovely, but there's nothing else like the playfulness of clouds—those dreamy gifts that come to decorate the sky. It's such a wonder to look up and see countless fluffy, wispy, thin, gloomy, and transparent shapes. I love to draw and paint them, and I even made a series of paintings called "Happy Clouds." It was a joy to begin to study these whispers from the sky.

Awareness of what's above you is a way to connect and ground yourself during a busy, hectic day. Look up and notice all the sky has to offer—rays of sunshine, a palette of colors, fleeting clouds, twinkling stars, and the waxing and waning of the moon.

Respect the Spirit of Place

Genius loci—the spirit of place—is recognized in many cultures as the soul of the land and its unique characteristics: native trees and plants, climate, water features, stone, topography, animals, and even the constructed environment.

A garden that complements and enhances this spirit will have a special quality that's felt immediately when entering. There is at once a sense of wonder and connection. Yet many gardens have been so artificially created that there is little left of the original atmosphere. The topsoil has been stripped, monotonous lawns and predictable plants have replaced the original wild landscape, and now there is little to distinguish one place from another. When you see such a garden, it's obvious how essential it is to be aware of genius loci and how much it differs from untamed Nature.

When you approach gardening as a cocreator with Nature, you see Nature as living and animate, a sentient being rather than a resource to control and dominate. And when you deeply love a place, you create a relationship of commitment and intimacy that awakens your indigenous heart and mind and strengthens your relationship with the Earth.

PRACTICE: Visit a local nature preserve or an old, still-loved garden, one where the planting and topographic features have not been disturbed. Look, listen, feel, and breathe with the land. Connect to the spirit of the place. What do you sense about the ancient and "uncivilized" land you are on? How can you use what you discern to establish and energize the genius loci where you live? In your own garden, use design elements that enhance the character of the place and respect the contours of your land. Reestablish native plant colonies, welcome birds and local fauna, and use geomancy or feng shui to balance the garden elements. Show respect, love, and commitment by recognizing the spirit of place in your garden. You and your garden will be blessed one hundredfold.

Embrace the Night

As cosmologist Brian Swimme tells us, we are all made from stardust.

PRACTICE: Go outside to the darkest place you can find and lay down under the night sky. Become aware of a living, expanding cosmos and our connection in present time and deep time—the multimillion-year time frame within which scientists believe Earth has existed. If you can see thousands of specks of light, put your hand up: The space of one fingernail will cover up one million galaxies. Think of the implications! You can't help but be in awe of the vastness of the night sky, reflect on the interconnectedness of life, and allow yourself to hold deep reverence for Earth.

The stars invite us to glimpse what is impossible to comprehend—the ever-expanding cosmos—right in our own backyard!

It is from the generosity of the stars, as they burn up and their light goes out, that life-giving carbon is released. And on a clear night sky, especially when there is no moon, we can connect to the stars themselves.

The night is a wonderful time to experience the garden—and some people even plant moon gardens, with silver foliage and white flowers, for warm evenings, romance, and celebrations. Planting with the phases of the moon is a traditional practice: Put in root crops (like carrots and beets) on the moon's wane, sending energy downward; install above-the-ground plants on the moon's wax, pulling them upward like the high tides.

The moon's phases synchronize you to your own natural rhythms, too, and it's a different kind of time tracking, free of clocks and calendars. The new moon is a time to begin new practices, and cultures across millennia have celebrated the moon cycles. Offer your important intentions in the full moonlight for blessings and unexpected rewards.

Stargazing links us to all people in all of time. Our ancestors looked at these same stars for guidance and story; future people, thousands of years from now in a world we can only imagine, will also gaze at them. If you have a smartphone, try the incredible app SkyGuide to view and identify stars.

Make Generosity a Habit

Because of salmon-rich rivers, gigantic forests growing on the edge of bountiful seas, and a profuse plant life of berries, food, and medicine, the native people of the Pacific Northwest had time to develop rich animistic mythologies and art forms reflecting that abundance.

They were so imbued with a true sense of plenty that they celebrated with a potlatch, a feast that centered on the giving of gifts. It was during the potlatch that claims of the clan and personal animal symbols were made, and totem poles were carved and erected in recognition of each family's guardian spirits. Like family crests, totem poles tell the story of the animistic powers and connections each family has, and in this way totem poles give them status and protection. They did not need to hold on to material riches to prove their wealth. It was judged by what they *gave away*.

Once, I was invited up to Haida Gwaii (formerly the Queen Charlotte Islands, British Columbia) for a thank-you potlatch that included all 850 people on the reservation. There was traditional drumming, dancing, singing, and feasting that lasted for hours. At the end of the evening, many gifts were passed out to each person. Then, as if that wasn't enough, the plates, silverware, and glasses used to eat with—and copious amounts of home-baked cookies, cakes, and meats—were all sent home as additional gifts. I had never experienced anything like it, and I was deeply touched and inspired. The Haida and other clans can teach us much about generosity, and with the abundance that so many of us enjoy, we would be wise to follow their example.

Gardeners are generous with sharing seeds, cuttings, tips, and the bounty of food and flowers pouring forth from their gardens. Giving comes in many forms (from offering possessions to listening and helping) and can be a part of every day.

PRACTICE: Reflect on the Haida value that status comes from what you give away, not how much you possess. Sort through your material abundances for things you can share or give away. Make donating food (whether garden riches or groceries) a goal each month. Plan a garden celebration to share your harvest and gratitude with your friends and community, lifting up the bounty with music. Your generosity will generate abundance.

Glean Wisdom from Trees

Mature trees connect us with the three worlds: to heaven with their branches, reaching into the sky or future; to the present with their trunks, solid and reliable; and to the underworld of our ancestors, our deep unconscious, and our pasts with their roots planted in the Earth.

PRACTICE: Sit with your back resting on the trunk of an old tree and quietly feel its energy. Consider the wisdom carried by the tree and its long history, from seedling to maturity, with all the wildlife and humans that have interacted with its trunk, branches, and canopy. If your garden has adequate space, I encourage you to plant trees in your garden. And cherish any trees you already have. An apple or any fruiting tree that goes dormant and then blooms and bears fruit in the spring gives a gift of great beauty and surprise from what appeared to be death. This connects us to the life, death, and life cycles. An evergreen tree becomes a beacon of well-being all year long, connecting us to an everlasting quality of spirit that is constantly renewing with grace.

It is extremely important to protect old trees and to develop personal relationships with them. To touch or embrace a tree is to acknowledge and feel all its life force just under the bark.

In ancient days, when people recognized tree spirits, it was customary to knock on a tree to awaken the spirits and ask them to reinforce a positive experience or intention. Today, when we say "knock on wood" for luck, we are recalling this ancient tradition. But trees are for more than just good fortune. The presence of trees lowers crime and lifts spirits; street trees bring peace. Wangari Maathai, from Kenya, won a Nobel Peace Prize in 2004 for the idea that human rights and environmental conservation are linked. In the 1970s, she founded the Green Belt Movement, inspiring thousands of women and children to plant more than twenty million trees to clean the air and provide shade, habitat, water, and cooking fuel.

I recently organized a community tree blessing with a Buddhist Rinpoche and an indigenous healer to stop the cutting of fifty thousand oaks along a stretch of the California coast for a "development." We sang, wrapped the trees in prayer cloth, and hung prayer flags. For the ancient Druids (and for me, too), oak groves are sacred. Oaks live for hundreds of years, offering their blessings of health and beauty.

Good Vibrations

Most of us have experienced sound vibrations when we hit a drum and put our hands near the source of the resonance.

There are many types of vibrations in a garden, too, and they bring forth a subtle but profound awareness. Plant vibrations are evident in healthy, happy plants. When plants are well placed and tended, a buzz of health permeates the garden. I first noticed this in Princess Sturdza's magnificent garden, Le Vasterival, on the coast of Normandy, France. I've made many trips to the Amazon rain forest in a pristine part of southern Ecuador, where there are no roads and no resource extractions, and where the forest is held sacred. Here, trees are revered, and I always feel the vibrancy of the jungle with the intact web of life—thousands of species of plants, animals, and insects living together interdependently. Every time I visit a garden with good vibrations, I experience a visceral feeling in my body, mind, and spirit because Nature is nurtured as mother and mentor, but not dominated.

I've also noticed when plants are stressed from disease, insects, or neglect. When I've visited Monet's garden on a Sunday afternoon among crowds of people, the flowers appear weary, as if they are tired and worn out, like hosts after a party. I don't photograph them—I just greet the flowers and wait until they are more refreshed and vibrant.

PRACTICE: **Enter your garden or a spot in Nature. Slow down and breathe with quiet awareness. Sense the vibration of the colors and sounds around you. Watch the interaction of flora and fauna, and see if you can perceive the vitality of the place. Be aware of the vibrancy of the plants. What can you sense from them? Are they healthy, do they need something, and do they seem at home? You can experience sound vibration in the garden, too. Put up a wind chime, listen to the wind rustle leaves, and hear the splashing in a birdbath. What sounds reverberate through your garden?**

"I do not know, but I *do* perceive." —Plato

Wabi, Sabi, Suki

Wabi, sabi, and *suki* are individual concepts that, taken together, are the essence of Japanese beauty—and the foundation of an aesthetic ideology that resonates particularly well with Gardeners who cherish Nature, artistic expression, and spirit of place.

PRACTICE: Where in your garden or in your life do you notice simplicity and subtle elegance? When does the patina of age bring more grace? Take time to walk quietly in your garden and find examples of wabi, sabi, and suki. Reflect on your life and areas to embrace this philosophical aesthetic. Is your front stoop well worn from years of visitors? Is your face showing some age, along with the wisdom and grace from experience?

This ideology embraces the loveliness of imperfection, impermanence, and the process of becoming and encompasses both the creation and the unraveling of something organic, rather than the staid perfection of something machine-made that will never show age or the artist's hand in its creation. For example, contrast the sense of soul and humbleness in a table handmade from driftwood with that of a sleek glass and stainless steel table, manufactured from manmade materials that show no hand of their maker. Both are functional, but they have different appeal, style, and design statements.

The essential elements of wabi, sabi, and suki are, respectively, tranquil simplicity, patina of age, and subtle elegance. Gardening as a spiritual path and way of life provides tranquility and expresses the wabi concept. When maturity creates beauty, as in an old garden with moss-covered stone walls and green terra-cotta pots, this mellowing reflects sabi. The suki element might be the change of light as it moves across the garden or fog drifting across the hills.

At seventeen years old, I was an exchange student in Japan and lived in a very traditional village between Kyoto and Nara surrounded by rice fields. There were no cars; the gravel paths were strewn with broken pieces of blue-and-white china. I was the first foreigner to stay in the village. The experience informed my eye, spirit, and soul for my entire life. I didn't know the concept until years later, but I knew the feeling. I came to realize that the wabi-sabi-suki aesthetic is a humble way of life, a path to follow that echoes Nature in form and ideology.

Water: Every Drop Precious

Water is the essential element for all of life.

With its ability to cleanse, purify, nurture, heal, and grow plants, it is sacred in all cultures. It represents fluidity, flexibility, resiliency, and yin, or feminine energy. Water connects us to Grandmother Ocean and water creatures. It mirrors the sun's radiance by day (the male sun god) and the silver light of the moon by night (the feminine moon goddess). Yet water is a precious resource, one that is in dire need of conservation and protection at this juncture. Do what you can to conserve and cherish clean water and its source.

A garden featuring water will attract birds, fish, animals, and water plants, creating its own unique and rich ecosystem. Water attracts children and adults, too, for play and serenity. Moving water, such as a stream, a fountain, or a waterfall splashing into a pool, will produce an energizing chi (energy) and a relaxing sound.

PRACTICE: In some places, we are experiencing great droughts. Use this as an invitation to redesign your garden for greater water sustainability. Abandon or conserve commercial water and instead collect rainwater by fixing rain barrels to downspouts. (Check with your local codes. In my garden, I have two immense tanks that collect ten thousand gallons of rainwater from my roof, which I save to use during California's long dry season.) Research further and discover the sources of your water supply. Where is your region's watershed and how large is it? Is your water sourced from a well, local rivers, lakes, mountain streams, or from some far-off place? Is your community doing enough to protect its water? Get involved, ask questions, and share the message that clean, healthy water is vital to the well-being of all.

"We never know the worth of water till the well is dry." —Thomas Fuller

The path of the

Artist

Expanding Your Creativity
and Imagination

As Artist, your creativity and imagination will be ignited, expanded, and engaged as you play and experiment with new mediums of expression. You connect to your heart and gain courage to face old fears and are no longer held back by old patterns of comparison or competition. You realize that being an Artist is a natural way to express yourself in all aspects of your life, from the way you dress and how you play to how you cook and plant your garden. You bring natural gifts of vision, innovation, and imagination into your lifestyle. As your imagination expands, you discover new ways to meet challenges, whether you dance, sing, paint, or write. As Artist, you become a skilled visionary and an alchemist. You immerse yourself playfully in the process of creating what has never before existed and upscaling what is not yet valued. You trust your ability to envision and live in harmony and balance without knowing exactly what those things look like. You practice initiating and leading creative experimentation with childlike curiosity, transforming mistakes into new possibilities. You welcome diversity to cocreate the best solutions for your own life, your work place, your community, and your environment. You work with passion and commitment for a better life. You embrace the idea that everyone can move beyond the status quo. You attract opportunity and fun, bringing unexpected beauty back into the world. You playfully engage your passions, integrating them into every aspect of your life. Inquisitive and awake, you welcome the creative tension that arises when you blend imagination and skill, creating something that has never been seen or experienced before. This process revitalizes and reweaves the fabric of your own life and that of your community.

Imagination is the magic carpet ride to the unseen, unknown, and yet inexperienced, transporting us from impossible to possible!

Art Studio on the Go

Once, I carried sixty pounds of art supplies into the Amazon and taught a school of Achuar youth to paint with watercolors.

PRACTICE: Make yourself a portable art kit. Take it with you for at least a week and make sketches of everyday objects (like your coffee cup in the morning). Doodle while you're on the phone. Draw as you wait for an appointment. You can add background color to your sketchbook pages by painting several pages with a thin wash of watercolor paint in various pretty colors; having color on the page makes it less daunting than beginning with a clean white sheet of paper. Try going out to the garden and priming the pages with soil, leaves, or flower petals. Or color pages with tea, coffee, or spices like turmeric. Then head outside with your portable art studio—to the park, to the scenic overlook, or around your home. Be spontaneous. Capture the moment. Express your mood.

They were natural artists and keen observers, and because they had no expectations of creating "fine art," they were able to express their creativity quickly with the simplest of tools. It made me realize that we can *all* take a lesson from this: If you keep simple art supplies nearby at all times—in your car, kitchen, or tote—then impromptu art-making is easy and accessible. You'll be surprised at how natural it feels to express your feelings and capture memories through art when you're at a beautiful place, see an amazing landscape, or feel an emotional bond to a moment in time.

Your traveling studio can fit into either a reusable plastic bag or something fancier and more durable.

Some basic items:
- **Soft drawing pencil, sharpener, and eraser (I prefer the soft putty kind)**
- **Black waterproof drawing pen or roller ball pen**
- **Small set of watercolor paints (try the Koi or Winsor & Newton travel set)**
- **Two small brushes (such as a pointed one for detail and a flat one for washes)**
- **Sketchbook or journal with heavy paper (spiral bound or accordion-fold allows pages to lie flat)**

More things to add:
- **Colored pencils (I like the ones you can get wet with water and create a wash)**
- **Oil pastels (an inexpensive small box is fine and better than crayons because the richer colors can be smudged and blended)**
- **Scissors and a glue stick for collage**

Ephemeral Art

Drawing can be a profound kind of meditation, especially when you draw slowly and observe very carefully. It becomes the Zen of seeing.

For my botanical illustration class in college, I once spent about 25 hours carefully drawing a common kitchen onion. I knew the onion so intimately that I think I fell in love with it.

Many Zen meditation gardens have meticulously raked gravel to represent pools of water and waterfalls—and they are skillfully recreated every day in a traditional form of ephemeral art. At a mindfulness retreat I attended on an Oregon beach, my friend Duncan Berry (page 162) led a group of all ages in writing sand calligraphy with bamboo poles and forming enormous and elegant spiral sand mandolins with rakes. Just as they were completed, the tide came in and erased them. They may have been temporary but the meditative process was imprinted on our souls.

Art is an expression of the human experience, and the process of creating is an essential ingredient. We don't need something tangible or long-lasting in order to be enriched by the journey. Look at the stunning transitory art of naturalist Andy Goldsworthy, which is made right in Nature of natural objects and recorded only with a camera.

PRACTICE: Select a simple form, such as a leaf, a pear, or words you like. Then spend at least ten minutes observing and drawing it. Go slowly, being mindful with your breath and really training your eye to see and direct your energy. You can make ephemeral art, patterns with salt, flower petals, or even sidewalk chalk. Try creating lovely patterns, carefully arranging autumn leaves or stones balanced on one another. Once you've finished, let it go and keep only the process and the memory.

Start a "foolish project." Art isn't "practical," nor does it have to be; it just feeds our soul and creates culture.

An Artist's State of Mind

If you wait until your life is in order, your house is clean, your food is cooked, and your bills are paid, there often isn't the time, energy, or impulse to create.

I greet you, beloved painting, with joy, confidence, and an open heart.

I deserve this time to paint and make art.

I source from the great pool of love and knowledge.

I source from pure creativity with gratitude.

Thank you from my whole heart for this wonderment.

I go through this distraction/procrastination process with every creative project—and need deadlines to set aside the siren call of "other things to do." But your limitations can be an asset, turning your lack of time, your need for money, or your physical constraints into motivators that can help you focus on your drive to creative expression.

Often, you need a ritual that supports you. For instance, Branham Rendlen, a painter from Big Sur, first puts on music (like Mozart) that inspires creativity in her. Then she recites an affirmation (at left):

It can take discipline to begin and be consistent, just like an exercise program, but once you are into the groove, your body craves it. If your creative expression is awakened regularly, your heart and spirit will call you to play.

PRACTICE: Select a piece of music that fully engages your attention and will get you into what I call a "no time presence," where you are deeply connected without distraction. To warm up, do some quick drawings or paintings that you don't care about. You might even put on a timer for five minutes and see what you can do. Then engage fully for twenty, thirty, or sixty minutes, without constriction or attachment to the outcome. The artist's state of mind is a process—start it.

Create an Artist's Journal

My journals are bulging with inspirational ideas, sketches from places I visit, visions I have collaged from magazine photos, childlike messages scrawled with my nondominant hand from my intuition, and more.

Dana Reynolds leads groups where individuals make their own "Sacred Life-Artisan's Book of Wonderment": She encourages artists to set sacred intentions, to begin with a prayer, and to allow their creativity to be blessed and guided by their own imagination. Artist Lita Judge (page 150) makes a healing journal with images, articles, notes, and photos that encourage her and make her happy. She looks through her book when she is undergoing difficult medical treatments.

Your journal can be a book of whatever has meaning for you—a record of what you love, a home base for your creative expression. You can draw, paint, write your dreams, or make a mosaic of your heart's yearnings and intimate expressions. You can also give shape to your inner visions, daily life, or travels with a collage from magazine photos or postcards. Your journal will be both a process you love and a time capsule of what inspires you right now—and an intimate companion on your creative journey.

PRACTICE: Use pages in your artist's journal for your own writings, reflections, and sketches. Cut out photos of yourself and add them, as a collage, into landscapes or paintings you love—then glue inspiring words and sentences over the photos and paintings. Piece together affirmations made from cutout letters and words. Work with spontaneity and intuition and be open to surprises as you gather together your life, dreams, and goals. As you add to your journal over the next few months or year, you'll be amazed by your insights and how many of your goals are realized.

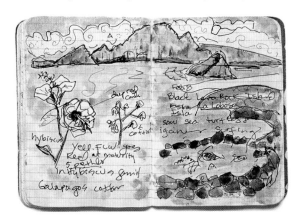

To create an artist's journal, gather these supplies:

- Blank journal or sketchbook (a black 11 x 14-inch spiral-bound book is ideal)
- Waterproof black pen
- Watercolor paints
- Colored pencils and pens
- Glue stick
- Scissors

Radical Amazement

As Artists, we walk a path toward creative expression that's uniquely ours.

PRACTICE: Find a place that amazes and awakens you. Look around and imagine that a blindfold has been lifted from your eyes. Are there new shoots emerging from the Earth—isn't that a miracle? Does that sparkle in the grass turn into a prism? Is there a tree silhouetted against the sky? Take the attitude that each moment, each view, is marvelous and full of delight and offer your gratitude. Observe and listen intently, then write a poem or make a sketch or water-color of what you're experiencing.

We go outward into Nature, seeking what deeply moves, touches, and inspires us, and then we take that revelatory spark and turn to an inward journey, connecting to our hearts and our souls.

Monet was once described as a pantheistic priest: He continually stood in radical amazement of the ever-changing light on his water lily pond. It was as if he were an alchemist, taking raw materials and mixing them with the fire of genius and awe to create works of art that transcended themselves.

When we are creating—whether it's a garden, a painting, music, a poem, even a recipe—we make a connection to a greater spirit of creativity. We are making blessed work. This process, which is more important than any art we actually produce, has been called *via creativa* by priest and theologian Matthew Fox. It, along with *via positiva*—which awakens awe and wonder in the joy of living—are both important aspects of making anything artistic.

I am always delighted and curious when I begin to paint, because while I have an idea of what I would like to make, what actually emerges is a surprising mirror to another spiritual and subconscious part of me.

Celebrate Beauty

We have become all too used to the commercialized definition of beauty: It's the cold, artificial attractiveness of perceived perfection in the smooth, Photoshopped face of a model that tells no story of her life.

It has fostered a vacant numbness in us, leaving us hungering for more meaning. Contrast that to the beauty of someone like renowned organic gardener Scott Nearing. When I was eighteen, I moved to Maine to put in a garden. Scott was in his mideighties at the time, still worked outside every day, and was my neighbor. His sparkling blue eyes were barely visible through the deep, sun-browned lines on his face. His charisma and integrity radiated out through his smile. He and his wife, Helen, lived a simple, handmade lifestyle, choosing to stay close to the Earth. Their values of truth and beauty have always stayed with me.

I think it's time to take back the notion of beauty. I often work in a soft, romantic style, and my hand-painted photographs were once criticized for being beautiful when beauty was supposed to be passé. Beauty is forever, and we can invite it to feed our souls and connect us to a radiant and unnamed spirit. True beauty asks us to pay attention and be present. Beauty is a blessing that visits us each day, an invitation to awaken to the sacred magnificence all around us.

I am honored to share the Navajo blessing "Walking in Beauty" here:

PRACTICE: Today, create something beautiful. It may be a simple flower arrangement in your home, newly planted pots on your terrace, or a more welcoming entrance. Celebrate what you've created, and notice how it changes the surrounding space and how you feel. And celebrate yourself: Look into the mirror with soft eyes and full heart and acknowledge your own beauty— without judgment or comparison.

May I walk in beauty.
Beauty before me,
Beauty behind me.
Beauty above me
Beauty below me,
Beauty within me,
May I walk with beauty
all around me.

Adorn Your Body

The body is the original canvas.

PRACTICE: Today, adorn yourself. Wear clothes with fun colors, textures, or patterns. Do you have a hat you like? Decorate it with ribbons, flowers, or a great brooch. Wear flowers as a crown or corsage, or just pin them to your clothes. Try carefully painting a pattern from Nature or inspired by tribal cultures on your hand, ankle, or face, or attach flower petals to your cheek with honey and experience how you feel.

For as long as we know, people have adorned their bodies to make themselves more beautiful and more appealing to the opposite sex. Body beautification is also used to show power, wealth, and religious status. It's fascinating to see people throughout history and around the world decorate their bodies with simple and rare objects of beauty—and to realize that, in the modern world, it is done for the same timeless reasons, but often with less handmade and more commercially available objects.

Some tribal people have tattooed themselves not only for beauty and talismanic protection, but to be recognized by their kin in this world and the next. The Achuar of the Ecuadorian rain forest paint their faces with different geometric designs—inspired from plants, animals, and birds—to welcome visitors, participate in meetings, go hunting or fishing, or to look more beautiful. With toothpick-thin sticks made from palm fronds, they draw designs on their faces with red, brown, or black plant dyes, which last from one day to two weeks. The Surma and Mursi peoples of the Omo Valley in Ethiopia are stunning body painters: They paint patterns on themselves and each other with colorful muds from the region and create elaborate floral headpieces with leaves, flowers, vines, gourds, and animal horns.

For Europeans, flower crowns were first used to emulate a person's aura. Later, to distinguish royalty, gold and rare jewels replaced the flowers. In the modern world, clothes, footwear, hairstyle, and makeup are common adornments, and tattoos and body piercings have become more popular. Each adornment can be a mode of personal expression and creativity, a way to celebrate yourself as an artist.

Create Community

Many artists are drawn to live amidst great beauty, gathering energy from expansive and natural surroundings.

Some inhabit gritty urban neighborhoods, upcycling dilapidated buildings with renewed vitality. Others make a place at the kitchen table when everyone else is asleep. But most artists form support groups for friendship, inspiration, and collaboration. Making art can be lonely. You're working by yourself and pulling truth out of your soul and onto your blank canvas, no matter the medium. Being authentic takes courage and soul-searching, and having support can make it fun and sustainable.

Almost any group can help support your commitment and invite collaboration. Away from the isolation of your own world and thoughts, you'll have the opportunity to share different approaches to the creative process—and have more aha moments. You'll expand in different ways. Classes, workshops, or spiritual groups that create together will help you go deeper and sustain your process. And all of you, as artists in community, will belong together in a space of imagination and innovation.

PRACTICE: Create an artist support community. How? Find inspiration among your friends and connections, and decide what will support you. Start with at least one person. Perhaps meet once a month in the evening with a like-minded group; everyone can show their art for a few minutes and share their process and goals. Then share a delicious potluck dinner or tea, and talk about your creative life. You could meet monthly for a walk and talk in Nature to support your creative visions, sharing your struggles and triumphs. Take a day retreat annually to set sacred intentions for your creative life. If your artist friends live far away, talk on the phone, Skype, or FaceTime to exchange ideas—then meet in person for intensive creativity. If schedules only permit calling or texting, send encouraging messages to one another. The practice of supporting another artist's creative endeavors—and being supported—will deepen your skills as an artist more than you can imagine.

Clear Up Creative Clutter

Like many people, I like to give myself permission to go into creative chaos and let things become messy in my process of writing, painting, collaging, making handmade books—whatever I am diving into.

PRACTICE: First, take time to clear some space—your studio where you create, your bedroom where you dream, your bathroom, your garage, a closet, a drawer, or even your gutters—anywhere you think energy is blocked and can't flow easily. If you have an art room, add shelves and clearly labeled bins to store supplies. Give away things you no longer need or use. Your generosity will make way for new energy and possibility in your life. You're preparing for the influx of vast creativity that's ready to shape the future. Second, state your intentions for each day, clearing your emotional clutter and focusing on a quality you'd like to embrace. Even setting out a clean piece of paper with ready supplies can get you going. Perhaps you'll say: "Today, I will make an inviting space to allow more room for creativity, and I will begin a new project."

Later, though, I find it takes discipline to clean up and put things away so there's an order to welcome me back. A space that is full of "piles of possibilities" can morph from a ripeness of creativity into dead energy that's just distracting. It's as if you have a fresh bouquet of flowers and then, after it has been sitting around too long, what remains is slimy water, droopy flowers, and piles of petals on the table. It is no longer energy giving and will actually suck up creativity. Too little chaos and we are restricted; too much and we can't create. Once distractions are cleared away, you have the literal and spiritual space for re-creation—your time to create, relax, recharge, revitalize, refresh, renew, rest deeply, and restore yourself.

Let's Dance

I once met a vivacious, beautiful young woman in one of my workshops.

She looked like a California surfer. I was stunned when she later shared that she had been in a near-fatal car accident a few years before. Her car had rolled nine times, and she'd injured her head, broken her back, and damaged her leg. She was told she would never walk again—but she knew that she would dance. Her passion for the tango, and that love of movement and music, gave her the courage and determination to endure many surgeries and physical therapy sessions to walk—and dance—with grace.

Dance is performed by every culture in the world as an important part of ceremony, ritual, celebration, and healing. The early forms of ecstatic, trancelike dances used in healing rituals are still relied on today in cultures from the Kalahari Desert to the Brazilian rain forest. Dance communicates and expresses emotions through movement, whether it's solo, with a partner, or with a group. It's an ephemeral art that invites us to be *in* the body, created entirely in the moment and leaving behind no artifacts. Dance is a cross-cultural way to show praise and gratitude in rituals like births, weddings, and deaths. In grief and joy, we sing, make music, and dance.

PRACTICE: Start getting into your body by standing with bare feet, allowing yourself to feel grounded and rooted, yet flexible, like a resilient tree in a storm. Begin to consciously move the major joints of your body, opening pathways that have been blocked from fear, judgment, and cultural conditioning. Next, playfully walk, moving all your joints and limbs. Picture exuberant African dancers who ground their feet and move their bodies fluidly, or hip-hop dancers who make powerfully sensual, liquid movement. Put on some music you love and move to it in a spontaneous, unself-conscious way, letting your body feel spirit and joy. Dance daily for health, vitality, and joy. You'll soon discover both pleasure and creativity in the rhythms of all your movement.

Dance is embodied emotion; there's joy, grief, or praise with each gesture, footstep, or beat.

Remember the Six Ds

Being an artist does not come effortlessly—especially with all the competing influences in our busy modern lives.

PRACTICE: Today, create delight by devoting yourself to your own creation with dedication and discipline. To begin, take out your art journal and, with a pencil, write some words of intention about your current desirable agenda. Then add color to your words with marking pens, paint, or collage. Make a commitment to do a magical page each day for a week. You'll be taking steps toward your creative vision.

But there are some qualities (all beginning with the letter D) that will make your artistic practice more focused and consistent, which will lead to increased creativity and joy in all of your life.

Discipline means to be your own disciple. It requires that you motivate yourself to be aligned with what you most desire to do—and obtain the skills that will contribute to your success. In an artistic sense, you are the clay that only you can form.

Devotion is the love, loyalty, or enthusiasm you have for a belief, activity, or cause. You might be devoted to your morning practice of meditation, a walk reflecting on your gratitude for your life, or doing yoga. Your morning devotion may be prayer or observance of your faith, or it may be time set aside to draw or practice your music. Whatever you choose, committed constancy will bring skillfulness.

Determination is a firm sense of purpose—a resolve and personal strength of character to keep steadfast to the vision of what you really want to create. This tenacity invokes a spirit of strong-heartedness to get you beyond self-doubt or a bout of procrastination.

Dedication may be a long stretch of hard work and resolve to accomplish your dreams. Caroline Casey, the great astrologist, mythologist, and storyteller, reminds us that "dedication magnetizes opportunity." You must dedicate yourself to the things you're passionate about.

Desire. What is it you aspire to create in your one wild life? What are you longing to bring into your life?

Delight yourself and bring pleasure to others by spreading bliss, beauty, and happiness with your joyful creations. When you create, your enchantment will captivate and inspire others.

Draw Playfully

As adults, we often have less confidence in, and are more judgmental about, our art. But when you let go of that, it's so fun to simply make marks on paper.

After all, drawing is a basic skill for creative visual form and communication. If you have not drawn since childhood, your skills may be at the same level as when you left off—so be kind to yourself.

Play some drawing "games" to break the ice.

Begin by just doodling while you're on the phone or drawing with your opposite hand. You can take a white candle stub and draw with it on newspaper—you won't be able to see your marks, so there's no way to prejudge yourself. Then, when you paint over the paper with watercolors, all your lines will magically appear.

Another inviting technique I love is to tape a black marker, soft pencil, or even a paintbrush onto a stick and draw from at least three feet away on paper taped to the wall or the floor. Matisse did this to create his large shapes, and when he was not well, he drew from his bed or wheelchair. With this method, you naturally make grand fluid gestures; there is no way to be tight and small and worried about details.

You can also try sitting across from a friend and drawing each other's faces without looking down at your paper. The first time will be funny, because all the features will be way off. As you practice, you'll get much better, as eye-hand coordination improves and you fall in love with the beauty shining through the face you know so well.

PRACTICE: Try a walking-meditation drawing: In your artist's journal or on a pad of paper, walk slowly in your garden, home, or other place you enjoy. As you walk, draw what you see—daisies, a tree trunk, the curve of some clouds, some distant hills. You'll get little sketch vignettes, and nothing will be finished. Your practice is really about deep observation, seeing what is in front of you, and drawing in the moment without a filter. And it's fun.

The true alchemical work is changing a piece of lead to gold. A humble lead pencil can be a magic wand, creating anything you can imagine—worth its weight in gold.

Heal through Art

It is healing to both create art and to be surrounded by its beauty.

✿ PRACTICE: **There may be a part of you that needs healing in the body or soul. Try working with some clay, building a little bowl from rolled coils or pinched from a ball. In your journal, paint a single flower or a scene out your window—the careful observation will be as healing as the act of painting. Consider creating a room in your home to be a healing environment, or help a friend create a healing space: Remove clutter, use soft natural light, place at least one flower in a vase, and bring in objects of simplicity, beauty, and usefulness.**

During Lita Judge's (page 150) arduous medical treatments, her doctor suggested physical therapy to strengthen her hands. When Lita showed up, all they had her do was squeeze balls in a hospital setting with other patients. As an artist, she knew she could do better using art. At home, she determinedly began working with clay, pinching together charming little animals. Over months of hard work, Lita's hands got stronger, and slowly she built stunning large pots from coils of clay. Lita believes "there is a bliss and joy found only in creating, more than just a relief from suffering." And most doctors would agree that happiness helps in our healing process.

When we lose ourselves creating, we can promote a positive mindset, reduce stress levels, and strengthen positive self-worth. And having art around us can make a huge difference: Think about the environment of different hospitals and how uplifting art can be. I've donated many large photographic murals of Monet's gardens to hospitals. I call them "Views to Healing." They become windows to gardens, and those who are healing can stroll right in.

For Monet, painting his gardens was a healing force during his elder years. Suffering from cataracts and lung cancer, he summoned the energy and determination to follow through on his extraordinary vision: He created his water lily panels as a "Bouquet to France" to help heal the nerves of his countrymen after the war. These paintings, which helped both to heal Monet's personal spirit and to give purpose to his life, not only soothed France, but also have continued to create a healing vibration for viewers even today.

Make Your Art Your Home

The Arts and Crafts movement was founded on the belief that our lives could be transformed by bringing beauty and handcrafted objects into the home.

William Morris's golden rule was "have nothing in your house that you do not know to be useful or believe to be beautiful." Morris, the aesthetic prophet, inspired the idea that the home was a reflection of personal style and that painting and design should be part of a social reform to restore the status of the artist.

But saying the words *home* and *artist* was difficult for me years ago because both ideas seemed elusive in my life. Now I realize I have always had both: It is when we feel at home in our hearts and lay claim to being an artist that the world opens up into possibility.

We can turn our homes into creative expressions of our personal style—as well as spaces where you celebrate and engage your inner artist. Your décor may include some of your own art, collections from your travels, or treasures you find from day to day. Try artistically mixing periods, styles, and textures with colors that you love. Select each piece for beauty, function, or at least a good story.

In my Celtic culture, like many others, hospitality is sacred. Any visitor can be the one to bring in unknown blessings—because, after all, your lover and all your closest friends were once strangers. The same is true for being hospitable to your creative and artistic self. Make your home beautiful and functional and invite friends to celebrate with you.

PRACTICE: **Start by looking around your home with the fresh eye of an artist. Try changing around the furniture to create a new look and feeling. Rehang wall art, providing good lighting (I like low-voltage tracks on the ceiling). Have a new piece framed and use it as a focal point. Consider reading a book about how to make specific spaces sing. I love** *A Pattern Language* **and** *The Timeless Way of Building* **by Christopher Alexander, who describes built environments and their "quality with no name" that you feel.**

Imagine

My late husband, Gerald Bol, was raised with this motto: If you can imagine it, you can make it!

PRACTICE: One way to loosen up your imagination is to let go of control and be open to surprise and spontaneity. Leave your routine. Try a new route home, dress wildly, change your hair, watch a foreign film. Imagine living in another place or time and what your life would be like. Eat exotic foods and picture where all those spices came from. Attend a cultural performance you have never experienced before. If you typically favor nonfiction, read poetry and fiction. Imagine a new story about yourself—change the perspective of your childhood, embellish facts, make yourself the hero or heroine—then tell it out loud in a spontaneous flow or write it down. Travel. Wander and be curious. You will be amazed by what you discover.

Imagination is listening when God whispers.

He came from a family of inventors, scientists, and artists—and imagination is just as important to creating art as it is for any invention. It can bring us to new worlds of possibility and potential. It's the fire that lights our will to not only create but go beyond what is known and accepted.

For the ancient Celts, imagination meant soul. John O'Donohue, a Celtic poet and theologian and one of my great teachers, always reminds me of this. Go into the wild and untamed realms of your soul, and you will meet your imagination—the well of all possibility that quenches your thirst and feeds your longing. It's a place that is always home for your true uncensored self.

We must behold and value our gifts, because imagination is not just for celebrated artists, writers, and thinkers. We all have it. When I teach creativity workshops, I often find myself saying, "Don't stick to reality. It is only the limited perspective of the moment." It is with our imaginations that we can go beyond our own perceived limitations and reach our true potential.

Inspiration

One of the origins of the word *inspiration* is this: the inhalation of Divine guidance.

In practice, it's an instantaneous flash of insight—with a sense of exaltation and delight. And most creativity is a mixture: an inspirational spark that starts the fire of passion, which then is sustained through the "chop wood, carry water" discipline of everyday real work. In fact, I find that gifts from the Muse come more frequently when I honor them by first writing them down or then acting upon them.

Inspiration isn't usually something you can schedule. It requires spontaneity and an inner trust. However, you can experience spur-of-the-moment creative flow when you speak from your heart and improvise in cooking, making music, dancing, writing, or painting. Improvisation is the home where inspiration flourishes. Each creative expression requires some skill and technique, but if you can surrender your ego while you're at it—and let go of outcome and addiction to perfection or "looking good"—something even better and more authentic will emerge when you least expect it.

PRACTICE: An inspiration board can be a place to collect and display images, words, phrases, or even directions that spur you to action. I use painted fiberboard attached to the back of a door. My friend, a historical novelist, tapes period photos and paintings on hers for each chapter theme, making it easier for her to picture her characters. Gather photos, magazine images, and postcards and collage them on your board or into your Artist journal to keep you on track. Track where and when you get the most inspired (along with what and who!)—in the woods, at church, among flowers, on a long drive, or with certain friends. Then go do it!

Lose Yourself to Find Your Self

Mary Holmes, an artist and art professor at UC Santa Cruz who died at age ninety, spoke of losing herself in order to really create and deeply experience art.

PRACTICE: Take time for reflection. What is your essence? What qualities make up your quintessential self? What could you let go of and still be you—maybe even *more* of the real you? Write down your thoughts and revisit the question periodically. If you had a dream life, how would you live, what would you do, and what would surround you with no limitations of money, time, or fear of failure? Allow yourself opportunities to go out and lose yourself. Attend a live performance of music, theater, or comedy; explore a new skill; or dive into a creative project to let your inspired self play!

When you are lost in music at a concert, enjoying a great play at the theater, or working away in the garden, you are no longer second-guessing yourself. You can get lost in your process. Nothing else exists, and yet you are joyfully present and open and in the flow. This is sacred time—a time when the Muse enters, or the Mystery, or whatever spiritual being speaks to you. Loosen your tight grip on control, let go of the impulse to compare yourself to others—even to a younger version of you. You'll be able to find your true, authentic, sweet, and vulnerable self.

When you lose an old identity—from illness, divorce, death of a loved one, loss of a job, or a move from a home or community—you are given a task: to find or rediscover your essential Self. My beautiful and beloved sister-in-law Pam sculpted glass with fire, played the piano magnificently, danced ballet for fun, and made everyone laugh with her great wit. At thirty-five, she was given the best news and the worst: She and my brother adopted baby Rebecca, and Pam was diagnosed with breast cancer a second time. She lost her long wavy platinum blonde hair but became the most dedicated mother. She lost her ability to dance or even walk, but spent hours laying with her baby in total love and presence. She gained clarity, strength, and a no-BS discernment. With little time and energy, she lovingly chose to be true to *herself.*

Welcome Your Muse

According to Greek mythology, Muses traditionally came in the form of nine women—with roots in the Earth Mother, the most creative of all.

The Muses represented many of the arts and sciences, from poetry and song to dance and comedy. It is believed that the Muses gathered together to share knowledge and created the concept of the *muse*um, a place for a*muse*ment, *mus*ic, and, of course, artistic inspiration.

My friend, chiropractor, poet, philosopher, and bagpipe player Ed Jarvis has a standing date with his Muse, whom he knows as Bridgette. Every Friday morning, Ed waits at his desk, wearing an Irish cap and holding a special fountain pen in his hand, and she inspires the poet in him. He honors the date, time, and place, allowing his lyrical poems to flow. He also takes off annually into the wilderness to be renewed by Nature, and to Ireland, his other great Muse.

I honor my own Muses by paying attention: I faithfully write down ideas to keep the channels open. I may be visited about a painting, a piece of writing, or a fount of new ideas. My greatest Muses are Nature and my playful, creative friends. I also like to write with my dog, Flora Bella, sleeping next to me. Lita Judge prefers her cat, Pu, sitting on her shoulder, or her small parrot, Beatrix, whispering ideas into her ear as she paints. Your Muse may be any sort of companion, real or imagined, as long as it inspires you.

PRACTICE: Sit in a quiet place. Perhaps light a candle or place a flower on your desk. Invite your Muse in, as a request, prayer, or intention. Begin to write a short note asking for guidance, insight, or advice for your creative expression. Then change hands and write whatever comes to you with your nondominant hand. Write down what you hear or intuit; don't question what you're thinking, just write in a messy child's scrawl. If you're feeling stuck while painting, give up control and use your opposite hand. Your Muse will likely intervene. You may choose to read *The Nine Muses: A Mythological Path to Creativity* by Angeles Arrien.

The Courage to Express

Fear can paralyze us, even when making art.

🌿 PRACTICE: **Quiet your critic with deep breaths and positive thoughts. Be curious and playful as you bring new energy and excitement to your creative life. Reach for the book *Art & Fear* by David Bayles and Ted Orland. Brush aside the fear. Sometimes just making marks with oil pastels on colored paper, and blending them with your fingers, will get you moving. Or try painting pieces of white paper with beautiful colors. Rip them into small shapes and glue them onto another piece of paper, making a mosaic. This action of simply painting fields of color, and rearranging them, will free you up. Stay open to the moment. Don't confine yourself with an outcome. Let it flow and bubble as you open up new artistic possibilities.**

"We have come into this exquisite world to experience ever more deeply our divine courage and light." —Hafiz

It can choke our courage and silence our voice. It can make us small and trembling; it can make us lose our confidence. We may no longer believe in what we love. We might judge ourselves, or others, too severely. Maybe we compare or imitate—or lose our unique vision.

I have been gripped by fear so hard I didn't think I could create. My way home is to breathe, slowly, deeply, and calmly. Over and over, I say a little prayer: "I love you. I believe in you." I connect to the courage in my heart, and it releases fear's icy, paralyzing grip.

Sometimes you must create like a mother of a newborn baby—tender, sweet, attentive, loving, and believing no matter what. It's almost as if you need to say to yourself, "I can't wait to see what you create, dear one. I love your process."

Other times, you need to be a warrior of the heart to protect your time, keep away critique, create boundaries, and believe fiercely in yourself. Show up. Get to work, even in the face of fear.

I once taught a creativity session of photography and painting. One of the students was a natural artist, but she told me that she had not made any art since second grade. Her teacher had criticized her art, and she had lost her confidence at such a young age. That day, she reconnected with her heart, overcame her fear, and created!

Flowers as Art

Gardening can be the highest art form and flowers an offering to connect us to the Divine in Nature.

We partner with Nature, using design, colors, textures, movement, form, scent, time, feeling, and purpose. What better way to develop being an artist than to garden, employing all senses over time? Gardens have inspired great art—like Monet's paintings of his transformational water lilies. "If it were not for flowers, I would not have been an artist," he claimed.

Flowers are used in all cultures of the world to beautify ceremonies, celebrations, and rituals. As many as sixty thousand years ago, Neanderthals offered flowers to the departed. For centuries, women have made flower garlands, wreaths, and pyramid-shaped arrangements for use on altars. Flowers have long been symbols of femininity, fertility, and ephemeral beauty.

For me, flower arranging is a sacred art, as if I'm performing a dance to inspire me to gather, create, and present. It's my favorite mode of creative expression. I often find myself in a reverent and prayerful mind-set, especially if I'm arranging for a wedding or funeral. I've been lucky to create with great flower artists, like Jeanne Cameron in New York and Thomas Gröner in Germany, where we have made enormous arrangements for flower shows, museums, and celebrations. I believe that flowers from the garden, grown with love, are noticeably more vibrant than commercial ones. They bring together individual beauty, scent, and love—a gift from the garden to the gardener. I must always have fresh flowers in my house to feel at home.

Flowers given with love never fade in the heart of the recipient.

PRACTICE: Collect some flowers in the wild or from the garden, a farmers' market, or a flower shop. Pay attention to the colors, scents, shapes, and where they grew. Make an arrangement for your desk, altar, kitchen, or dining table. Notice how the feeling in the room—the vibration—changes. Make a little handheld bouquet for a friend. You'll be giving a small gift of joy.

Finding Your Song

Every culture of the world plays music and sings songs.

"Watch for all that beauty reflected in you and sing a love song to your existence." —Rumi

I've learned from my teacher Angeles Arrien, a cultural anthropologist, that the drum simulates the heartbeat and bells bring joy, awakening us to our life dreams. Rattles mimic rain and are used in soul retrieval work. Click sticks can be used to stop repeating negative family patterns. Songs have been sung since the beginning of time to express love and sorrow, comfort children, and rouse warriors to hunt or fight. Songs can connect us to higher spirits, help us to stand behind a country or a cause, and inspire us to celebrate and to praise. Music is a way to build community and bridges between cultures, ages, and backgrounds. It is an expression from the soul, and voice is our most natural musical instrument.

It's still very mysterious how music works and moves and opens our hearts and souls. There is a science to musical acoustics, vibrations, resonance, and harmonious chords, and these rhythms can inspire us to dance, to rest, to pay attention, and to wake up.

PRACTICE: In some African cultures, each person has a unique song, created by mothers for their children-to-be. Sung from birth to death, in joy, sorrow, trouble, or illness, the song brings the individual back to his or her own true self. Now, create your own power song. Angeles Arrien suggests you use your own name at least three times, telling a story of your character qualities. It's best if you can make up your own melody, but feel free to use a familiar tune and rhythm. Keep it simple and make it yours. When you sing your power song, notice how it centers you and gives you confidence to be yourself.

Nature as Your Mentor

Jay Harman picked up a spiral shell on the beach, and from that, he invented a new fan that saves energy.

Monet painted the light, and in that fleeting moment, the Impressionist movement took off. Nature can teach you everything you need to know about creativity, invention, and innovation. Just observe the change of light, the effect of colors on leaves, or the sky throughout the day from dawn to sunset. The diversity of living forms, trees, mountains, oceans, rain, wind, flora, and fauna that make up the matrix of life itself can mentor you.

I have been greatly inspired by the new science that informs us of the ever-expanding nature of the cosmos. And as an artist, you can tap into this as an ever-expanding possibility of your own ingenuity. The more we are aware of the diversity and creativity of our own planet, the more we can find ways to be mentored in our own artful expressions.

Intimacy with the land is characteristic of indigenous peoples' relationship to their ecosystem. It is natural to know where your water comes from, to be attuned to the ripening of foods according to the seasons, and to live in balance with your environment. Living with balance and reciprocity is the basis of all creativity and respect. Spending time in Nature will develop your skills of observation, improve your health, and fill your spirit with the impetus to create.

"God's Revelation is nature. Man's is Art."

—Henry Wadsworth Longfellow

PRACTICE: Go outside and choose a shape, like a spiral or a circle, and find out how many places you see it—in the whorl pattern of a sunflower, in a snail shell, in the way branches go up a pine tree. Can you incorporate this idea into the design of a painting or a flower arrangement? Mix watercolors to match the color of a flower, or make a collection of fabrics or yarns that remind you of your garden. Breathe in the beauty and ask that it comes through you, mixing in your heart and out your hands as you paint, photograph, or write.

Notice, Appreciate, Discern

I come from a family of world travelers and collectors.

PRACTICE: How do you train your eye? Try this morning routine: Open your eyes, look out a different window than usual, and notice the light, weather, and something new about how the day arrives at your home.

Visit a museum or art gallery and sit quietly in front of a painting, to practice seeing. Spend an hour in your library looking through art books that you've never pulled off the shelf before, or look at a favorite artist's work that has evolved over time. Find an artistic treasure from a tag sale. Seek out gallery shows beyond your comfort zone or visit exhibits showing objects you're not familiar with. Attend a high school or professional play in a culturally diverse neighborhood. Whenever you have the opportunity, travel! Being in a new place awakens your ability to notice, appreciate, and discern immensely.

Our mother—an artist, a Nature lover, and a spiritual seeker—trained us six children very early on to have an eye for beauty and quality. She helped us to notice light, drifting fog, sparkles on the bay, and wildflowers blooming in the hills. With many trips to museums and auction houses, she shared her love for design and form and her appreciation for diversity in art from different cultures. My own study of Nature and botany trained me to see the details in plants, birds, and landscapes that have been essential for appreciating and creating paintings, photography, and gardens.

Our mother also encouraged us to find things of beauty even from flea markets, way before it was in vogue to shop secondhand. My brother Jim restores old houses. His eye for proportion and his intuition for how a space will work are astonishing. My brother Thomas is a world-renowned collector of tribal sculpture and textiles. He says, "Art is my passion and spiritual connection with the outside and inside." As a teenager, he learned from Carlos Castaneda's book about Don Juan, a Yaqui shaman, that the difference between "looking" and "seeing" is the key to discerning. Thomas has looked all over the world with a keenly discerning eye that's connected to heart and meaning. He can truly see.

Paint

Painting can be the love of your life if you allow yourself to play, experiment, and stay curious.

However, if you compare yourself to others and try to paint like them, it can also be painful. The key is to make sure you foster openness and invention. How do you start? Try experimenting with process painting—it's when you concentrate on the *doing*, not the outcome. It will loosen up and deepen your authentic voice. I like to use water-soluble tempera paints on large sheets of white paper mounted on a wall, and I work in meditative silence, following my impulses without preconceived ideas or rules. Stay curious and see what emerges—shapes, figures, splotches, patterns. When I was grieving, this type of expression, without language, opened up healing channels to my heart and spirit rather than closing down.

When you paint from what is inside your imagination, not from what you see with your eye, you create a doorway to a new world that both you and a viewer can step through. If you're intimidated by the idea of painting, just mix rich colors you love and apply them to paper. That alone is magic. Henri Matisse used to "paint with scissors," cutting or tearing brightly painted papers to make a collaged painting. You can also go outdoors and try plein air painting, capturing the immediate light of a particular place. Concentrate on colors and shapes, and don't fret about the fine details. Your love of place will bring you in touch with the spirit of the land, and that is an essential part of the experience.

**For a juicy life: Abandon judgment,
play with color, paint for joy!**

PRACTICE: In your artist journal or on paper, try one of these styles of painting:

- Paint what emerges from your uncensored subconscious impulses ("process painting").

- Paint outdoors in your garden or in Nature, paying attention to the light and the exact shapes and colors you see (plein air).

- Paint from a playful place. Be open, experiment, and allow yourself to express what you feel and see ("inside out").

Try Photography

I first fell in love with photography at twelve years old when Uncle Fenton handed me a medium-format view camera from Japan to photograph his party.

PRACTICE: Photography can be used as a chronicle of your life journey as well as a meditative tool. Try taking at least one photograph a day for a month or even a year—whether it's your garden or objects in your home that you love. Explore with a new eye, seeing as if for the first time. Experiment with different perspectives. Perch on a high vantage point, taking in the whole for a sense of place, then take in the details with some close-up vignettes. *Miksang* is a Tibetan word meaning "good eye." It has inspired a whole approach to contemplative photography to capture the essence of what you see when you are present. Photography can be a spiritual experience—as well as visual communication. You can share with friends online and print your best images for notecards or for the wall.

Looking into the camera, I was a part of, yet separate from, the action. I was there to witness and capture the familiar with my own point of view.

The camera (or phone) can capture travel, changing seasons, or fleeting moments of precious times with family. It used to be known as "drawing with light," and looking at paintings can teach you a lot about composition and light. Photography invites experimentation—in what you photograph, the technique you use, or how you print. Sometimes I like to print on heavy watercolor paper and then paint over the photo with pastels and oils. It's a multimedia creation with amazing results, even for beginners.

Today, thanks to technology, we can all be photographers. "iPhoneography" has captured my imagination, and I process images in my hand with different apps—it's endlessly creative. You can generate sepia tones or something painterly, and you can immediately share it with people of all ages. I teach painterly photography and now iPhoneography as a creative process that sharpens the eye and opens the heart to beauty, as it awakens the Artist within each of us.

Remember to Play

For all of us, play is simply about being totally in the moment, in the pure joy of process, with no concerns about outcome.

It's important for us to loosen up and have fun. Play sparks creativity and encourages risk taking. Play helps us accept and even welcome change. It stimulates curiosity. To create, we must continually adapt, invent, and respond. As we experience wonder and possibility, play also causes us to adjust and find new ways of doing things. We can accept that life is about change, process, growth, and flexibility. *Lila* is a Sanskrit word that means "divine play." It is the play of creation, destruction, re-creation, and love.

Even businesses and places of work are realizing that play is important for creativity and personal well-being, and sometimes that manifests in computer games that develop the whole brain. Play theorist Brian Sutton-Smith says that the opposite of play is not work—it is depression. Just think how common depression is in our workaholic society. Think, too, how humor brings joyfulness, laughter, fulfillment, and a deep satisfaction with life.

Unstructured play in Nature is the best kind of play for children and adults. We can use our imaginations to make things up; we can innovate; we can create whatever we feel by trial and error. Improvisation is just another form of play, and it's a wonderful way to make music, do stand-up comedy, and create art. When we play, we feel energized and happy and have a willingness to embrace the unknown.

 **PRACTICE: Go out and have some fun. For you, it might be trying a new recipe, making a messy painting, or revisiting an activity from childhood. You may enjoy sports, golf, or Frisbee. Play charades with friends after dinner, or get out some musical instruments (like rattles, bells, drums, guitar, ukulele), put on some music, and dance. Give yourself permission to be free and wild and unrehearsed. Invite friends to play with you, to share laughter, imagination, and joy.**

When we venture into play, curiosity trumps self-consciousness and our joyful engagement drowns out any critics.

Writing Poetry

Poet David Whyte says that in poetry we overhear ourselves saying things we didn't know we knew and that poetry is a soul dialogue, as if life's mystery is speaking to us and through us.

PRACTICE: Begin a word palette. Look through books, such as art, poetry, or old garden books, finding new and interesting words, and then list them in a notebook—or write them on little pieces of paper and put them in a jar. Use them to compose some verses. It's like adding new spices to your pantry and experimenting with them to expand your cooking. Read poetry out loud to inspire your own rhythm of language and use of metaphor (my favorites include Mary Oliver, Pablo Neruda, Rainer Maria Rilke, John O'Donohue, Naomi Shihab Nye, David Whyte, and the Persian poets Rumi and Hafiz). Listen to poets reading, either live or recorded. Then write a poem, haiku, sonnet, or prayer.

> "Know that there is often hidden in us a dormant Poet, always, young and alive."
>
> —Alfred de Musset

Poetry can heal the heart and awaken soulfulness in our own voice. I know several doctors who are also poets, and they actually prescribe writing and reading poetry as a healing practice for their patients. Words said aloud or silently have resonance that can shift our feelings, thoughts, and even biochemistry, bringing healing and creativity. The rhythm, breath, and sound connect to heart, mind, and spirit. A poem expresses something in a distilled and refined manner, to be savored and sipped slowly.

I find myself writing poetry when I want to express the essence of an experience. It helps to create what I call word palettes—a collection of luminous words to use like the colorful tubes of paint that inspire my art. I keep my eye out for words, as if I'm searching for them like sea glass on a beach. Then I take them out to play around with, creating sacred prayers or healing poems.

I asked my poet friend John Dotson, "Why poetry?" He replied, "Poetry works in mysterious ways—ultimately unknown and unknowable. Something happens in poetry that takes us to our deepest origins, our roots, in rhythm, in the pulse beat of an irretrievable past. Poetry has magic that we don't understand, while leading us to greater understanding, greater awareness, and connection. A world without poetry would be like a world without birdsongs or ocean waves or fog flying over the face of the moon."

Taking the Leap

The artist is a risk taker.

When you create, there's a probability of an uncertain outcome from your effort. It could be a new recipe, a sketch, or the first pages of a novel. No matter what, it's always a leap to get started.

Years ago, I hired a well-respected contractor to build a cottage. I was stunned when, on the first day, he looked at the plans and said, "Well, I'm going to have to figure out how to do this!" It was a revelation for me. I always thought that I had to figure things out or adjust them as I went along because I lacked skills; I realized from that moment that not knowing is part of the creative process. And the way is revealed in the process of creating, in those tense moments of *not* knowing, guidance comes.

Courage allows you to take risks as an artist, to trust your own inner voice or intuition, to follow your inspiration, and to express what you love. Each time you take a risk, you're inviting curiosity and building sufficiency to override your frustration of not being instantly "good." It's humbling that artistic skills take time to develop, and most of us are not instantly good at something new. I have found that consistent patience, combined with humor, is most helpful. The plunge is always worth it.

Of course, there is a risk of not being accepted or valued, but the greater risk is losing your soul from not ever trying. Have the courage to live a life true to yourself and not the life others expect of you.

PRACTICE: Self-doubt often comes from fear of failure or fear of looking foolish. Try to notice what ignites your own lack of confidence, and write a specific positive verse, affirmation, prayer, or *gatha* (meditative verse) to return to your creative center and help you overcome confusion and self-doubt. Then make a list of some things you would like to learn or do creatively that you have never done before. Pick one and begin with experimentation, a class, a workshop—or ask a friend to teach you. Sometimes all you need is to begin.

open to outcome   adjust   patience

get started   courage   trust

Tell a Story

I have been enthralled with stories since I was a child.

PRACTICE: Once a year, I attend a workshop led by therapeutic story-teller Nancy Mellon, and I love this exercise, which you do with a part-ner. Look softly at your partner and feel his or her essence. Then tell a story about your partner's magic cape or shoes or other prompt—you describe what it's made of, what it looks like, and the wonders it per-forms. It's so surprising to hear what comes from your imagination and how it helps your partner see his or her unique qualities. Take turns, enjoying a story told just for you. For the children in your life, tell a story from your own childhood. It will nourish them and deepen your relationship.

My Uncle Fenton sailed the South Seas, bringing sailor's yarns and treasures from Asia. We six kids would gather around him, and he'd tell us about his adventures sailing a junk around islands that had never seen a European before, about the typhoons he'd survived, and about the enormous anaconda snake he had tripped over in the jungle and then killed, boiling its skull to keep. He was our guide, transporting us to foreign lands, helping us form a world view and a hunger for adventure, exotic foods, and strange customs. We hung on every word and asked questions as our imaginations flickered with images more dramatic than any in cinema.

The landscape of story took root in each of us. We had some tough times in our childhood, and the family tales fed us and rooted us to a landscape we could journey in and navigate from. They were a pass-port to our ancestors and to other worlds—real and imagined.

Textiles for Art and Healing

Knitting and stitching can be highly meditative, therapeutic, and productive.

Take the Knitting Behind Bars program. It teaches men in a Maryland prison how to create hats, dolls, and other small items for their children and people in need. Along the way, it gives them new skills, improves self-esteem, and encourages patience. The connection shouldn't be surprising. Textiles have always been deeply meaningful, woven with a profoundly spiritual motivation, sometimes in weaves fine enough to be buried in and taken to the next world. Even when more sophisticated looms became available, the most sacred cloths were woven on the simple and archaic backstrap loom by both men and women.

Once, I had a dream that my late husband Gerald's love wrapped me in a pink embrace. My friend Margaret Moore heard about my dream and spent a year weaving me a shawl in pink mohair. The very day I received the shawl, I was on my way to have a second surgery for possible breast cancer. I insisted on wearing my pink shawl. The procedure was halted because I kept fainting.

That same day, my dad died. I arranged the flowers for my dad's funeral, and during all the rituals, I wore my pink shawl. Later, I stitched spiral patterns onto it, and as my needle went in and out, it centered my thoughts on love and blessings. I found embroidery to be a meditation, and I began to wear the pink shawl for meditation and prayer. When I returned for the rescheduled breast procedure, the lump that had shown up in many mammograms was no longer there.

PRACTICE: If you already knit, quilt, or do needlework, you know that it centers you. Stretch further and try a more advanced or new skill. If you're new to fiber arts, wander into a yarn or fabric store and sign up for a class. Enjoy the sensuous textures and pick out something you love. Knit or crochet a hat, make a patchwork pot holder or pillow, or even try embroidery as a meditation. Learn to appreciate textile art. Visit the library and pull books on tribal textiles, vintage sewing, tapestry, patchwork, or costume design over the centuries. It's a fascinating glimpse into incredible handmade art across the globe.

The path of the
Lover

Opening Your Heart
and Falling in Love with Life

On the path of the Lover, you will fall in love again and again with commitment and joy. You are willing to fall in love daily, fully engaged in life. The Lover taps into an ever-renewable source of the infinite, ever-expanding cosmos. As Lover, you embrace the power of universal love, and you release the fear that constricts you. You create new covenants to value and care for all relations—human, animal, plant, and mineral. You commit to protecting what you love, bringing compassion to your community and responsibility. When your heart opens with love of your family, place, faith, and calling, you naturally prioritize. You work hard and do what it takes to move forward and succeed, making adjustments in your lifestyle to support and nurture what you love. You take a stand for all the children and their children in future generations. You love and honor the elders and listen to their wisdom as you bridge respected traditions to the best of current innovations. You lead from your heart with gratitude, grace, and love-centered commitment as a model of a new way of living. These practices will assist you in transforming life's challenges and losses into gifts and feelings of gratitude. Some practices will help you heal a broken heart and become open to joy and loving kindness. They will invite you to intentionally connect with what has heart and meaning and to courageously take risks to follow your passions. Here you deepen your authenticity through vulnerability and intimacy, allowing yourself to be truly seen, to be loved, and to love openly. You gain strength as you practice forgiveness, connecting to your roots and feeling support from your ancestors. As you follow what you love, the clarity of your life's purpose and true calling comes into Full Bloom.

"Love the world as your self; Then you can care for all things." —Tao Te Ching

Living on Purpose

To live on purpose means bringing your unique contributions to the world as a meaningful offering of service to something greater than yourself.

PRACTICE: In your journal, list all your gifts and talents, from languages you speak to parenting skills. Don't be modest! These are your assets. Then list what breaks your heart: children in need, climate change, illiteracy, animal rights, health inequality, civil unrest, inadequate elder care—the list could go on and on. Consider how you could contribute to changing that. This is your compass and fuel for action and gratification. Anything on these lists may reveal one of your purposes.

Every person has a purpose in life, maybe several. To follow your calling entails this: connecting with your passions, working in alignment with your heart and your spirit, and contributing to what has deep merit and meaning in your daily life.

I think our world is shifting from an economy based on gross national products—making things that depend on resource extraction from Nature, lots of advertising, merchants, consumers, landfills, and wars—to a global community that wants to derive happiness from meaning, beauty, and spiritual depth. And as it moves in that direction, work becomes focused on service in support of life and taking care of land, people, and soul. Finding and following your calling or bliss—as mythologist Joseph Campbell so famously suggested—is the greatest opportunity for a meaning-filled life on purpose.

To find your calling, sometimes you have to be confident that there *is* a higher purpose, and that being a disciple to yourself in times of uncertainty and great need will make you come fully alive. You must lean in and listen to the whisper of your heart when you can't sleep; take time to contemplate your deepest intentions as they reveal themselves to you, whether you're playing an instrument, sitting in reflective meditation, writing in your journal, or weeding in the garden with dirt under your nails.

Find Your Passions

What opens your heart and makes it sing?

That's your passion—it's a fire within you that's often stoked by love, and it burns bright to show you your unique way. Just like fire, it can be the fuel to provide life-sustaining energy and vitality. Your passion might be an abundant and raging bonfire, or it might be a little flame that needs to be carefully stoked. But it's there, in everyone.

I was recently teaching Life Mapping to a group, and when I asked everyone to list their passions, a shy older women said, "I have no passions." So I asked her, "What do you love?" She brightened right up and said, "My grandchildren!" As she thought about them and the rest of her family, other loves begin to emerge. I found out that she was a retired scientist, a great cook, and a proud homemaker. She loved music, gardens, and everything about children—hers and everyone else's.

Identifying your passions gives you a place to move to—like a distant mountain you want to hike—and your awareness, strength, and desire will help you find the way there. Of course, some people have a lot of passions, and they spread their gifts to many. Others focus and develop depth with just one idea. Once passions are identified, it's important to figure out how best to cultivate them and identify the obstacles (perhaps many of them!) you'll face. Like any hero's journey, your creativity and commitment will get you through.

PRACTICE: In your journal, list your passions and great loves in life. What sustains them? How do you stoke your fire—is it time in Nature, meditation, or being in the garden? Passion brought to others creates compassion. Whom do you feel compassion for? Can you commit to doing something *every* day to stoke your inner fire?

"Someday, after we have mastered the winds, the waves, the tides and gravity, we shall harness for God the energies of love. Then for the second time in the history of the world, we will have discovered fire."

—Pierre Teilhard de Chardin

Honor Your Ancestors

Ancestors and others who have gone before you help you know your life story.

PRACTICE: What is your relationship with your ancestors? Do you know your family lineage and cultural background? Have you traveled to the land of your grandparents? What values and traditions do you want to cultivate and nurture? Consider dedicating a space in your home to honor those who have gone before you. Hang framed photos of your family in a special place at home. For an anniversary or birthday, light a candle and say your loved ones' names out loud, place some flowers in remembrance at a favorite spot or resting place, and ask for their guidance when you face decisions or struggles. You may find that you feel comforted by the presence of loved ones daily or at special times.

They usually are relatives, by birth or marriage, but they can also be teachers or clan members who shaped who you are. To know your ancestors is to root yourself in your culture and family lineage. After all, you are the fruit of the tree sown and tended by your grandparents and great-grandparents long ago. It's humbling to remember and acknowledge all the love they had and hard work they did to make it possible for you to be who you are today.

Some people believe our loved ones on the other side can be powerful intercessors, like saints in the Catholic Church, who offer us strength and guidance. In Western, Eastern, and Earth-based traditions, there is a shared belief in an afterlife where ancestors exist beyond death. These different practices connect families to loved ones who have died—and encourage kinship and stories. Some families keep altars in their homes and make daily offerings of food, flowers, or incense. In some cultures, late October to early November is considered the time when the veil between our world and the other side is thinner. All Souls Day, All Saints Day, Day of the Dead, and Halloween are celebrated then, and it can be a good time to be open to the energy from your ancestors.

If you believe in the spirit in all beings—the plants, oceans, and four-legged creatures—then your lineage and connection may extend beyond humans. You can be open to and receive guidance from all forms of life. If there are any family patterns you want to break, ask them to stand behind you as you courageously change. Creating a ritual of respect and honor can change your relationship to the past and to your future, enriching your present. The best way to honor ancestors is to emulate their best qualities and look after their legacy by caring for the Earth so future generations will honor your lineage.

Learn from Animals

Since time began, people have had close relationships with animals: in the wild as a food source or threat, as a spirit totem connecting us to other higher domains, as allies, as domesticated work animals, or as companions and pets.

When I see a rare wild animal, I think of it as a blessing. And I'm not alone. Many different interpretations of animal totems are found in all cultures of the world.

Science tells us that if we're near an animal we love, like a cat purring next to us, it can lower our blood pressure and increase our sense of well-being and relaxation. If a pet does something that makes us laugh, it can promote healing in a joyful way. Therapy dogs are used in hospitals, airports, and prisons, and they have made a positive difference in the lives of abused children—and, of course, have given independence to the blind.

It is a privilege to be close to and develop relationships with animals. They express unconditional love, courage, and empathy. My dog Toolie was a close companion for 17½ years. After my husband died, Toolie patiently reminded me to tend my own animal body by eating, walking, and playing. He stayed by my side when I wrote, painted, and worked in the garden. In his older years, his calm and loving presence was like living with a peaceful monk, strong in spirit and wise with intuition. His simple life and calm breathing was a meditation. Like all animals, he was a wonderful example of the power of unconditional love.

PRACTICE: Perhaps you are fortunate to have a pet. If so, find ways to spend more time playing and learning from one another. Try to listen to what your pet is communicating to you. If you don't have a pet, visit an animal shelter to see if you might want to volunteer. Or develop a relationship with a friend's pet. If you're able, try to observe animals in the wild and celebrate their diversity and interconnection.

Nurture the Children

My mother used to say, "Children are gifts from God, and each one is a flower in His garden."

 **PRACTICE:** Pick a little bouquet with a child, and talk about the scents, tastes, and textures of plants that you love. Make flower or leaf crowns for you both to wear and feel the magical delight, or dig in the soil to find earthworms and insects. Plant some seeds, like pumpkins, so that children will come back again to check on the plant's growth. Have something to nibble on in the garden, harvesting the bounty together. Children love to make little accordion-fold books and fill them with leaf and bark rubbings, pressed flowers, Nature words, and paintings done outside. Tell them a "once upon a time" story of your childhood memory in the garden and how you came to know Mother Earth.

Because she planted a different kind of tree for each of her six children, we grew up rooted in the Earth—relating to our personal tree and learning life's lessons with it. After a storm, when branches broke off the tall, more brittle trees, but not the weeping willows given to my twin sisters, we experienced the lesson about flexibility and nimbleness in life. The apple tree was my favorite, connecting us to seasons, offering us fruit and requiring pruning for best growth.

Each child requires nurturing and specific care to thrive. By loving the children in your life and valuing their welfare, education, and health, you contribute to their well-being—and to the future of the world. And we adults benefit as well: Though play and imagination are seen as the domain of childhood, they are essential to the well-being of all of us. Invite a child to play in your garden or out in Nature, and offer guidance, insight, and knowledge.

At a library storytelling event in a troubled community, I told a trilingual creation myth from the Achuar people to about one hundred Hispanic children and their mothers. Afterward, I offered to paint their faces with brown symbolic brushstrokes, just like the Achuar. With each eager fresh face, I felt myself falling in love. I could feel how their open hearts were full of possibility. A little boy said, "I want to be a warrior!" I told him, "That means you are a leader. I will paint you with energy from a jaguar for bravery and strength." I painted a shy little girl as a butterfly, for transformation and beauty. I felt my heart expand with love and appreciation for the precious gift each child is. Whether or not you have your own children, you can reach out to nurture children in your family, church, or neighborhood.

Embrace Your Elders

Spending time with elders can be a great gift not only to them but to yourself.

It's time to bring forth a collective respect and honor for elders and to embrace both their wisdom and our own aging process. There is much to be learned from those who are older than us. It can be difficult for many people to discuss aging and death, but we miss out on the rich lessons and familial heritage if we avoid conversations about growing old.

Don't allow fear of loss or fear of obligation to get in the way of your love and the precious gift of time you can share together. My beloved friend and mentor Kathleen Burgy was ninety-three when she died. We met when I was fifteen, and she guided me spiritually to stand for what I believe in. She used to say, "I love what I have. I use it up and let it go!" When she died, her body was like a tattered autumn leaf. Every time I missed her and wished she were alive, I thought of the wonderful story *The Radiant Coat*, which tells how the beautiful coat we are given at birth wears out, and at the end, we leave behind the rags and release our radiant spirits.

But before we go, we have much to offer. My world-traveling Uncle Fenton was eventually confined to a wheelchair in a care home in Florida. He focused on what was right, playfully bringing cheer, humor, and curiosity to his life, and giving compliments to other patients and staff. He brought joy to himself and others each day, and right before he died, he had a lineup of friends there to say farewell.

"Still bearing fruit in old age, still remaining fresh and green."

—Psalms 92:14

PRACTICE: Sit and talk with an elder, whether a family member, neighbor, or someone else you know. Slow your pace, share some tea, listen with an open heart, and practice kindness and compassion. Ask questions, be patient, and keep your humor. You may be surprised to learn their life story—a story of hardship, privilege, risk, or reward—and you may be overwhelmed to find how rich a life they've led and how much wisdom they hold. Seek out more than one person advanced in years. If you are lucky, you just may end up with a dear friend and a role model for how you'll want to be as you age.

Cherish Your Friendships

My greatest wealth is my friendships.

PRACTICE: Who are your friends? Real friends? Childhood friends? Casual friends? Acquaintances? Do you have friends of different ages and backgrounds? Make a list of some of your closest friends, and write down the essential qualities you admire in each of them and reflect on what you share. Expand your list to include other friends from your past or present, and identify what you have in common. Think about rekindling old friendships or cultivating new relationships. Then, take a step toward making friendships a priority, even when you're busy with work and family. Call several friends to check in on them and make specific "play dates" to have fun together. Plan a party, potluck, picnic, or tea, and help each other rediscover the joy of friendship.

They form the fiber of my being. They are the touchstones in my life, my support rafts in storms, and my playmates. Friends are the mirror that reflects back to us a fresh view of who we really are. Friends are our chosen family. As one of my friends says, "You're like my sister but without the baggage."

I have always embraced a diverse circle of friends and have nurtured them with time and love. Today, I have friends in a ninety-year age range, and they have a variety of life experiences, passions, and spiritual beliefs. For me, children bring spontaneous delight, youth are full of new ideas, peers have years of wisdom still to share, and elders impart an inspiring legacy. Midwestern friends have stability, East Coasters have more tradition, and West Coasters are full of innovation. People from other countries bring riches of language and customs into my life.

One thing we have in common is our love of celebrations! As I look at years of photographs, I see art projects, travel, and parties. And whether they are picnics, potlucks, or extravagant sit-down dinners, cooking together and creating the setting are just as fun as the party. Together we have celebrated weddings, births, and funerals. We have brought flowers and food, helped each other move, listened to challenges, and advised on love, finances, and career. Many of us share a passion for art, Nature, adventure, and spirituality.

Give Thanks

My friend Lynne Twist says, "What we appreciate appreciates."

Gratitude harvests the essence of our life experiences. Like sunshine and time, gratitude can turn a bitter fruit into a ripe, sweet, and juicy one. Conscious gratitude helps you to appreciate all you love in the world. It lends perspective to challenges and disappointments, fosters compassion, and transforms experiences into wisdom. Letting the gratefulness you feel overflow into each day is like quenching your thirst with cool water or warming yourself with sun.

When I was in college, I worked at an elementary school as a teacher's assistant. The mentor teacher I learned the most from would compliment all the good actions of the children, recognizing them with sincere appreciation. Her method transformed the class and me. When you give a compliment to someone, recognizing and appreciating their service, skill, or contribution, you'll see how it makes them light up. We all yearn to be appreciated.

PRACTICE: Watch Louie Schwartzberg's stunning time-lapse film *Nature. Beauty. Gratitude,* with its precious, heart-opening narrative by Brother David Steindl-Rast. He is a Benedictine monk who will help you open your eyes to all the beauty and gifts of each day and will help you to feel gratitude for all blessings of each day. Sign up on Gratefulness.org for daily quotes on gratitude and virtual candle lighting rituals to offer thanks. Read Angeles Arrien's book *Living in Gratitude.* Just before going to sleep, think about what you are grateful for today. At year's end or on a special occasion, reflect on a year by counting your blessings. I like to write down my favorite gratitudes in a journal, to read on my birthday or New Year's Day to celebrate the year; others write them on small pieces of paper and put them in a jar to read when they need a lift. Above all, remember to say thank you each day for the life you have and all the goodness that comes your way. It is the shape-shifter for negativity and the most potent antidote for woes.

When we count our blessings and offer our gratitude, miracles happen every day.

Live in Loving Kindness

Research shows that acts of kindness not only benefit the person who receives the kindness but also release endorphins responsible for feelings of contentment in the person offering the kindness.

PRACTICE: A simple daily act of kindness for yourself, for someone else, or for Nature will do wonders for your mood. Can you commit to thirty days of kindness? For yourself, set aside time in silence to affirm your life's path, to recognize your courage in trying something new, or to acknowledge being just the way you are. Forgive a mistake. Take time to walk outside and notice beauty, or just rest in a peaceful spot. For others, find small, simple ways to offer love, support, and encouragement with notes, calls, sharing food, doing a chore, or bringing flowers. For Nature, invite in wildlife with garden plants and birdseed, or give to causes and charities that work to restore habitat and diversity.

"Be gentle and kind
Seek peace of mind."

—Margot McKeon

In fact, Nature has hardwired us to be kind! This reciprocal gift makes kindness a joy for everyone. I like to think of kindness as gardening: You plant seeds when you are kind to yourself, and you water them with love. Each day, you nurture your garden by asking to be safe, healthy, and happy, and you can share in the abundance of kindness you have cultivated. You can set aside time to walk or sit in meditation, drink tea, bathe, or work in this "garden." Weed out any comparison or judgment of yourself or others, deliberately shifting your thoughts and actions. Your garden of loving kindness will bloom abundantly, and your seeds will spread.

Kindness to others could be many things: welcoming new neighbors, or being patient and understanding by letting a young mother with toddlers go first in a grocery line. You could bring a meal and flowers to an ill or busy friend. Your kindness will be as healing as any medicine. You could tuck a little note into a child's lunch or under the pillow, send a text message of love and encouragement to your mate or friend, or mail a handwritten thank-you note. Extend your kindness to Nature: Try feeding wild birds, stop for wildlife crossing the road, or compliment a blooming flower on its beauty. Extending yourself with acts of kindness to other people and beings brings you into blossom.

Fall in Love with Nature

I have found that spending time in wild Nature is the clearest mirror of my *own* true nature and a pathway to renewal and spirit.

Get to know one place well—a trail, a source of water, or even one tree—and you will fall in love and discover that everything is connected. Nature embraces us with the grandest of beauty, hospitality, and diversity. Just think about the landscape, plants, animals, sea, sky, and ever-expanding cosmos. Nature is generous and renewing, and I feel indebted for these awe-inspiring gifts.

My dear friends Ellie and Patrick are avid birders. Binoculars sit on the counter. Their bird-feeding station is just outside the kitchen window. Bird-watching is as natural to them as preparing food from their garden for dinner. Recently, we traveled together to the rain forest in Ecuador, the Andes, and the Galapagos on a Nature adventure trip. We set out at dawn one day to sit in silence for hours at a clay lick, waiting for the arrival of rainbow parrots—surrounded by Nature, in keen awareness, listening and observing. It was like sitting with my Buddhist friends and following our breath. This was a birder's meditation. When the parrots arrived, it was a gift of presence, like a flash of insight connecting us to the daily magic of what deep ecologist David Abrams calls the "more-than-human world"— what goes on beyond our usual perception and attention. I teared up.

I was just so much in love. In the presence of the enormous kapok tree, where we sat two hundred feet high looking over the entire canopy, I was stunned by the beauty of the location. At the sight of toucans and bright turquoise-blue *Dacnis*, I felt joy and excitement. I loved—and love—it all: learning about birds, trees, habitats, cultures, medicinal plants, and animals. In an intact ecosystem, you really see how everything is interconnected and how it is everywhere you look.

PRACTICE: Discover new insights into your own wild nature by spending time outside. Explore different times of day, from predawn to night stars. How do you feel in different ecosystems—the forest, ocean, desert, or mountains? Experience silence, expand your perception, and listen for Nature sounds—birds, wind, rain. Go on a quiet walk and look for feathers, stones, fallen leaves, shells, or beautiful seedpods. They might inspire a poem or a drawing someday or find a place on your altar.

This Moment Only Once

Being present can mean being present for others, being present for yourself, and being present to all that surrounds you.

🌿 PRACTICE: **Think about single moments—joyous or challenging—that changed your life. They passed your way just once. You can choose to hold on to them by placing them into what John O'Donohue calls "your tabernacle of memory," a sacred place that forms the fabric of your being. Or you can release them, letting them go as naturally as autumn leaves that were once a part of your life.**

Our presence is the most precious gift we can offer someone, and it requires deep listening that comes from the heart as much as from the ears. Your presence says: *I see you and affirm you. I hear your pain, I witness your heartbreak, I celebrate your joy.* When we can offer our presence to another, we are actually offering the space to be both vulnerable and authentic. And, in turn, our heart blossoms even when it breaks open.

For yourself, being fully aware of *this moment only once* is as simple as it is profound. Presence is the basis of many spiritual practices, teachings, and mindfulness trainings. Because you know a single moment is fleeting, you naturally open your heart wider to take it all in, breathe in, and then hold your breath as every cell is filled. You're inviting (and allowing) beauty, love, and happiness to fill you up. Even the most precious, treasured, and anticipated moments slip into the next ones. Celebrate the beauty and joy of this transitory moment, whether it's the beauty of a sunset or the joy of a baby's smile.

When my beloved sister-in-law, Pam, was dying, we all breathed with her in her long, uneven breaths. We, her sisters, breathed in and held the moment—then, as she let out her breath with a rattle sound, we joined her. In the emptiness, we wondered, would it come again? We were all united in the commitment of taking in life. We did this in unison about three times, and then Pammy breathed no more. Those precious moments of breath together, sharing the same air, had passed. That moment happened only once, but we were there completely, and none of us will ever forget it.

I am here holding your heart as I get nourished with your presence. I offer you my presence, all fresh, all new, all for you.

Be a Fierce Warrior

Love sometimes requires the strength and commitment of a warrior: You must take a stand and protect what you care for.

Every parent knows this feeling when it comes to their children. The vulnerability of babies requires putting their care first and being on constant guard for their immediate well-being, as well as thinking of their future. When my husband became ill, I felt like I had to be both a fierce watchdog and a devout, tender protector, both nurturing him and advocating for what was best for him.

Love is deeply connected to heart and values. The Achuar people in Ecuador were known as fierce warriors, bravely using blowguns and wit to keep invaders out of their pristine rain forest for thousands of years. They are the keepers of their forest home, and it has benefited all life on Earth. Today the Achuar have transformed their warrior commitments to be great leaders, working with others to establish rights for Nature in Ecuador's national constitution.

It is essential to know what you love and what you stand for, because then you know what you're willing to fight for. The Earth needs each of us to take a stand and be a warrior for what we love: our own children and *all* the children, our land, trees, water, air, and natural resources. You matter to this world, and what you love matters to this world. It will impel you to make commitments to protect the precious things around you, to make adjustments in your lifestyle when necessary, to be strong, and to be a leader when you identify a cause you're passionate about.

PRACTICE: Think of when something you love comes into your life—a new baby, a puppy, a new garden. Remember how you have to nurture and protect them, bringing commitment and adjusting your priorities of time, resources, and daily actions. What actions are you willing to take to protect what you love? Then take this fierce care and direct it toward a new cause or an opportunity to affect change (whether it's water, soil, food, animal rights, or anything else). Can you deepen your knowledge or teach or inspire others to join you? Could you share your awareness with your community, club, or local school? Learn about what it means to give rights to Nature in Ecuador's constitution and what that would mean where you live.

To be a warrior of the heart: Spend time in Nature, fall in love with your life, and take a stand for what you love.

What You Love

Do you know what you love, what really makes you happy, and what you value most?

🌿 PRACTICE: **I find that the process of filling a book with collaged images made from personal photos, magazine cutouts, and quotes is both insightful and joyful. Take a double-page spread to explore a theme like home. What is it you love about it? The garden, a room, an activity, or a place you go back to for inspiration? (For me, it is France and Maine.) Show photographs of natural or built aspects of this place that enrich your life. Devote pages to exploring your family, friendships, and spiritual beliefs, with photos, quotes, poems, stories, and artistic work. It will become a time capsule of your life and a reminder of your experiences, convictions, and commitments.**

The process of finding the images and words in magazines, and your own collections, will be enjoyable as you assemble each page with the theme you have chosen. There will be a sense of calming and affirmation as well as joy that will seep into you. It is more than a scrapbook. It is a pictorial journey into your mind and heart of what brings you happiness and what you value.

What you love describes a lot about who you are and, most likely, how you live your life. When you are unclear about what you love, you can get wobbly and indecisive, taking a long time to make a choice and often second-guessing yourself, even when faced with questions as simple as what to order at a restaurant. If your decision is about a job to take or leave, a relationship to cultivate or weed, or how to spend your money, what you love is essential to helping you figure it out. It will also help you discern areas you may want to define, deepen, and clarify. What you love can be your compass as you navigate your life's journey and solidify the values you wish to hold. Your love list can be long, broad, and inclusive, as well as ever-changing. Your heart will expand, and your life can be guided by what you love.

"Let the Beauty of what you love be what you do." —Rumi

Make Commitments

What you love you commit to—a life partner, the country you live in, family, spiritual beliefs, work, or Nature.

Commitment is being dedicated, responsible, and engaged. It can be a promise to yourself, a legal contract, or a code of ethics you live by.

I admit that I once felt commitment-phobic. Making commitments seemed too restrictive and confining, and living without them gave me a sense of great freedom and possibility. But I finally realized that it is impossible to have clarity and depth without commitment. Only by taking a stand did I receive the discernment and structure necessary to direct my own life compass. I could navigate my life more purposefully, and my creativity, relationships, health, spiritual depth, and happiness bloomed.

When I take groups to the rain forest or teach Life Mapping, I invite everyone to make a commitment bundle and articulate and share commitments. Commitment bundles are based on a tradition I learned from Angeles Arrien, who used popcorn, rice, or beans to symbolize how many commitments you were making and would actually act on. Creating a ritual of commitment that is spoken and witnessed by others is both moving and life-altering.

PRACTICE: Light candles and, in silence, invite yourself or a group to consider what commitments you want to make. Spread out a fabric square and place in it the elements that will support your commitment. Tie your bundle closed with string or ribbon. When you've finished, everyone is invited to state aloud the commitments they will take action on daily for thirty days. All who are present will be sacred witnesses to support you. Dr. Arrien says, "What you witness you are changed by, and when you are witnessed, you cannot go back to the old way."

To make commitment bundles, you'll start with:

- 3-inch squares of fabric
- String or narrow ribbon for tying

Then you'll need some ingredients to place inside:

- Seed, like popcorn or beans (to symbolize each commitment you will plant and nurture)
- Soil (symbolizing a commitment to Mother Earth)
- Rose petals (symbols of love)
- Thyme (a symbol of time, because we must set aside time for our commitments)
- Rosemary (symbolizing remembrance)
- Pearly everlasting flower (for its perpetual quality)
- Cinnamon sticks (symbolizing the sweetness in your commitments)
- Coins (to put money behind your commitments)
- Leaves (what you're willing to let go of)
- Other local ingredients that make literal and symbolic sense
- Paper (to write your commitments on)

Communication That Matters

One of my great mentors of clear communication is Patrick O'Neill, who runs a business called Extraordinary Conversations.

✺ PRACTICE: If you're trying to communicate with someone, listen first. Remember what is being said. Then speak from your heart and tell the truth. Angeles Arrien and Patrick O'Neill teach that if conflict arises, speak up—ideally within three hours or twenty-four hours, possibly within three days, but don't wait more than one week. When it is time to speak, choose the right time and place that both can agree on, and come from inner stillness rather than reactivity. In other words, during a period of intense communication, a reflective pond is more effective than a raging river—just keep the flow.

Patrick works on levels from intimate relationships to international conflict resolution, leadership development, and team building. He is a great tracker, following what is said like a hunter noticing paw prints. When he listens to others, he remembers what and how something was said and communicates with thoughtful integration and sharp insight. His use of humor diffuses any tension and provides the flexibility needed to see another point of view without attachment and defensiveness. This is as important with family members as it is with colleagues, friends, or opposing countries.

Patrick succinctly sums up the four qualities that support excellence in communication and leadership:

- *Sufficiency* leads to integrity.
- *Integrity* leads to responsibility.
- *Responsibility* leads to right relationship.
- *Right relationship* leads to sufficiency.

"Right relationship" comes from the Quakers, and it means living with honor and respect for others. I began attending Quaker meetings when I was fifteen, where we meditated in silence until we were "moved to speak." These were not conversations but clear messages of inspiration that required deep listening and inner quiet. It taught me to reserve judgment and avoid comparisons to others, and to be open yet discerning. Most of all, it taught me to be present, to listen deeply in that moment, and to discern true inspiration.

Communication can inspire greatness and weave community with deeper clarity and intimacy. With compassion and right relationship, we can reach understanding, transforming conflict into empathy.

Courage and Encouragement

Courage is the capacity to be connected to your heart and to have the determination and conviction to follow what has truth and meaning for you.

In Latin *cor* means "heart," and we have come to define courage as bravery. Both are required to do something that might be painful or frightening or bring disapproval. Courage is one of the most essential virtues: You need it to practice all the other virtues consistently, from doing original art to saving someone in a burning building to listening to a friend's fears on her deathbed. Ernest Hemingway famously defined courage as "grace under pressure."

Courage requires the intention and dedication of an athlete to keep the heart open, strong, and clear.

We *all* need encouragement. To encourage someone is one of the sweetest gifts of friendship, mentoring, and humankind. With your encouragement, you support others in connecting to their heart and finding their fortitude to follow their path and stay motivated. Humor can be a wonderful way to encourage, bringing fresh perspective and illumination and lightening the load. Encouragement is like getting out a flashlight and helping a friend who has become lost in darkness or despair, and is frightened, to get back home. When you believe in people, they can again believe in themselves.

PRACTICE: Think about times when you've had to find courage to continue—with a job search, with a physical challenge, with a goal, with a new relationship. Your courage could have been with true bravery or with your personal convictions, creative expressions, and life choices. How has being courageous enriched your life? Who has motivated or inspired you to be courageous? Track how you have been courageous. Plan ways you can turn your courage into encouragement for others. Choose three people to encourage and support—at work, among your family and friends, or even strangers you meet. Talk with them, see where they are on their journey, and offer words of encouragement from your heart.

Be Curious

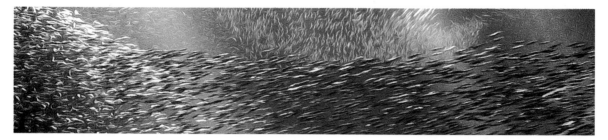

Curiosity keeps your mind and spirit open to new possibilities and opportunities.

PRACTICE: Curiosity is a playful way to get you out of feeling stuck. Order something totally different on a menu, take a new route home, or ask about your family history. Head to a local museum, open a cookbook to a new page, or track down a childhood friend. Be curious about your body, rather than judgmental. Be more open and adaptable in relationships by asking about needs and feelings. From the close up to the faraway, curiosity will expand your world and point of view.

Like a traveler or anthropologist meeting and observing a new place and culture, curiosity keeps you flexible, open-minded, and free of judgment. With relationships, as with all creative processes, curiosity brings you into the realm of possibility where everything can be considered. Contemplating the what-ifs is expansive fun. Being open to discovery is the way of the explorer and scientist—and it will bring delight, love, and appreciation into your life.

But you don't have to go big. You can be inquisitive about something as familiar as the way your body moves as you're walking down the street or while you're doing yoga. Or you might become curious about your moods. What makes you happy, or what knocks you off-center? Stay curious as you track yourself and others. Think to yourself, "Hmmm, that is interesting!" rather than "Hmmm, that is wrong."

Being curious can help to change your point of view. Children are motivated to learn and inquire; they are always looking for new stimulation and exploration. Look at the world through their eyes and keep that perspective as you grow older. As a youth, I became a "junior scientist" at the Steinhart Aquarium in San Francisco, which ignited my imagination. Later, I loved visiting churches and temples and was intrigued by the different ways to practice spirituality. I have always been interested in different beliefs concerning God and afterlife. Curiosity keeps me open and free of judgment and comparison.

Depth and Clarity

If we only looked at the top of the sea, we would never know the wonders of its depths, the fish, the beauty, and the connection to all of life.

If we always stay at the surface of places, emotions, and subjects—what I sometimes think of as "drive-bys"—it won't cultivate intimacy. Clarity allows depth to be seen, and together they form confidence and trust, which lead to commitment. The ability to go deep with clarity of vision, purpose, and direction is a vital skill for crafting a life of meaning.

Depth, like digging a deep hole to plant a tree, takes time and some effort. Clarity requires focus and the right lens—wide angle, close up, or zoom—to get different points of view.

I love so many things and am so curious about learning that sometimes it can be difficult to choose a path to really focus on. When my friend Duncan Berry and I first did the Life Mapping process (see page 185), my maps were overflowing with long lists of my passions, skills, talents, and ways I wanted to contribute to the world. My great challenge was to find the North Star for navigating my life. Duncan suggested I work with depth and clarity, so I committed to it for a year.

Even three years later, "depth and clarity" is a mantra that help me decide what to do and what not to do and how much further to go, whether it is with an art project, meditation, or a pastime like snorkeling. My personal path of guiding people to lives of meaning, contribution, and joy is the outcome of several years of Life Mapping—with clarity and depth as my personal compass.

PRACTICE: Consider something of merit to you—a decision you have to make about a relationship, work, or your spiritual beliefs. Depth with clarity is the ability to see beneath the surface for previously unnoticed qualities to appreciate and discern. It requires attention, focus, presence, flexibility, choices, and the tenacity to follow through on those choices. Investigate your subject deeply by finding out details, asking questions, and listening more. Give yourself time to contemplate and feel it in your body, listen to your intuition, and pay attention to your dreams.

Treasure Your Family

I come from a big family with three brothers and two sisters.

PRACTICE: Acknowledge your family—large, small, related to you or not. Send a note of gratitude, make a call, or plan a gathering. If there has been a rift with someone, consider how you can make amends. I have found that sometimes more time shared doing something mutually enjoyable is a good place to start, adding to the positive experiences together. With kindness and humor, you can discover your kindred spirits and realize that the concept of family can embrace everyone.

Five of us were born within four years of each other! When our mom got sick, we raised each other, taking on different roles and responsibilities. At three, I could help feed my twin baby sisters, and at eight, I would get up in the middle of the night to feed my baby brother. He felt like *my* baby, and if he had a rough night, I would fall asleep in second grade the next day. But this was not a burden to me nor did I question it.

What does it mean to be family? Relatives share bloodline, ancestry, culture, traditions, and memories. There are many types of families—the family you were born into, the family you've created by friendships, the family at your job, and the family that includes other species. Through blood, marriage, or choice, we hold a special loyalty, intimacy, and lineage with family. And family members can be some of your greatest allies, teachers, and challenges.

But family life doesn't always turn out the way you expect it. People you love die or divorce; sometimes it's hard or impossible to conceive children; sometimes those children aren't born healthy; sometimes families do hurtful things. Each family experience shapes who you are, and in most situations, the diversity of outcomes brings richness, depth, and more meaning to life.

Once, I attended the Gathering of Nations Pow Wow at the University of New Mexico Arena. When a young man won best dancer, the announcer asked his parents to stand behind him. Then all his relatives were invited, then teachers, neighbors, and friends. By the end, there were more than one hundred people dancing behind him, some wearing feather headdresses and others with cowboy hats and baseball caps. I was deeply touched to actually see who stands behind just one person—and how family can mean so much more than just our relatives.

Be Flexible in Mind and Body

In this time of so much change, it behooves all of us to maintain our flexibility with our bodies *and* in our thoughts and views of the world.

We need to stay open to possibilities as we evaluate situations and ideas and adjust to new life circumstances.

Being flexible in body means movement comes easily and without pain. It means having fluidity and well-being. Yet flexibility takes consistent practice to stretch and condition the body. An exercise like yoga, dance, or walking increases strength and balance in body, mind, and spirit, bringing you the freedom to move nimbly without rigidity or attachment to your position. When you can be like bamboo, rooted yet flexible, you will be able to bend gracefully in the winds of change and not break down.

A friend's mother went to bed with grief after the death of her lovely adult daughter. Each day, she stayed inside with her curtains closed, not interested in the light, news, or even the lives of her grandchildren. Nothing could get her to leave; she became rigid and bitter. When she finally got out of bed, she could barely move her body; her limbs had become solidified, and she remains in a wheelchair, locked in the past. She is no longer able to move in the present moment without great pain. Each of us must walk a path through grief at some point. If we can remain flexible and accepting, we will deepen our wisdom and compassion.

The ability to be flexible, literally and metaphorically, is essential as we mature in our bodies and in our points of view. It is crucial to remain open to change, to aging, to loss, and to new possibilities with ourselves and with those we love.

PRACTICE: **Start a physical flexibility practice to stretch your body with pleasure. Try yoga, Pilates, dance, Nia fitness, or swimming to get embodied joyfully—whether it's at a gym or community center, or at home with a video or book. While taking care of your body, engage others in your classes, discuss different points of view, or tune in to a podcast to guide you while working out at home.**

Be Authentic

As a child, my mother's favorite word was *integrity:* the quality of being honest and having good character, principles, and ethics.

PRACTICE: **Can you name someone you know personally or historically who is authentic? Make a list of their character qualities and track how their ethical or moral compass has steered their choices. What can you learn from this person? Home in on how you can develop your authentic self. Who or what circumstances have been your teachers of authenticity and vulnerability? Write an affirmation or "Zen sticky note" (see page 139) to strengthen your own qualities of authenticity.**

Integrity comes from the Latin *integer* "to be whole and complete." She taught us to be honest, sincere, and truthful. It took me years to deeply understand what it meant and even longer to incorporate integrity into my character.

Our mother wanted to give us the confidence to be authentic. An authentic person is consistent: saying what you mean and doing what you say brings reliability and accountability. She wanted us to be "rugged individuals," capable and distinctly individualized yet bonded together to support one another. We were encouraged to question everything from religious doctrine to politics, learning to think for ourselves. Our education was to spend time playing in Nature on our own, to appreciate and create art, to work hard, and to travel the world.

I like to think of authenticity as the confident, bolder sister of vulnerability, who can be more quiet and shy. They go everywhere together. Without vulnerability—and a truly deep sense of self—authenticity can become arrogant or stubborn. Together, authenticity can mean a confident, truth-telling, and reliable character. You can count on yourself and others who are authentic, because who you are is who you present to the world. There are no masks that hide your true self and none of the baiting and switching that is so devastating in relationships, politics, and spirituality. When you are authentic, you are faithful to your internal compass for guidance—rather than trying to please, appease, or manipulate others.

Let In Vulnerability

Vulnerability is being at home with your true self.

You are comfortable to show up authentically with your open heart. Vulnerability comes from having inner strength (and is very different from the scenario of falling apart at the seams and collapsing in tears when you have pain or a tragedy).

Being vulnerable is a path to your own soul. It is not weakness of character; it comes from courageously navigating the labyrinth of your life. Awareness of it brings gifts of both beauty and humility that eventually lead to self-acceptance. We all have highs and lows. Who expects their roses or fruit trees to be in bloom the entire year? When you believe in yourself, you can let go of perfection and the need to look good—which requires control of everything. When you trust the rhythms of your own seasons, you can welcome sprouts, swoon over blossoms, delight in juicy fruit, and rest when all is dormant.

Navajo weavers intentionally create a small mistake so the spirits can enter and depart. When an old Japanese bowl cracks, it is mended with gold and becomes far more valued for its beauty. I think the biggest gift in being vulnerable is embracing your flaws and being a clear channel to give and receive love.

PRACTICE: Sit or stand in a quiet place, close your eyes, and imagine you are a great old apple tree. You are deeply rooted, yet vulnerable to extremes in weather and time. Using your imagination, feel your life-sustaining connection to the Earth. You have stood many years, rooted yet flexible, making light into food. You have been well pruned, and now your many limbs are ladened with fruit. Every year you have seen sunlight, rain, and wind as well as nights with sparkling stars and moonlight. Imagine yourself as this tree—vulnerable to change, yet strong and clear in this moment. You have survived hardship, yet you are more abundant from judicious pruning, and your blossoms and fruit come like grace. You, who connect heaven and Earth, now in your own authentic way, share your abundant fruit.

Cultivate Intimacy

Angeles Arrien says intimacy means "into me see."

✿ PRACTICE: Use a mirror to look deeply into your eyes. Say, "I love and appreciate you just the way you are."

When you're ready, ask yourself:

When I look at myself I see . . .

What I want others to see is . . .

What I don't want others to see is . . .

What I want others to experience when they interact with me is . . .

What I love and admire about myself is . . .

Allowing yourself to be truly seen takes courage—a connection to the heart and a kind of bravery that stands for what you know and love and believe in. It's your essential self.

And it's usually found in the company of authenticity and vulnerability.

To cultivate intimacy, the ground of trust must be well worked. You have to weed out any false selves, masks, or roles so you can accept yourself. One of the deeply tender openings to intimacy appears when you are really sick—or when you take care of someone you love who is terribly ill. The illness brings an immediate vulnerability that most of us don't like to show. The authentic self shines through—a bit of humor, a kind heart, an appreciation—as you offer or accept the homemade dinner, a ride to the doctor, or help in the bathroom.

Intimacy with others comes from knowing, accepting, and loving yourself. When you give the gift of allowing others to truly know you, you open the door to deeper bonds between your family and friends. Intimacy deepens rapport and establishes mutual confidence and dependability. And when you're intimate with yourself, you open up your deepest secrets and fears. Ten years ago, every nerve in my body was in pain, my spine constantly went out of alignment from muscle contractions, and doctors didn't know what to do. In desperation, I took the suggestion of an intuitive massage therapist who said my body was trying to "hold it all together," but I still had old grief and anger to release. I began using a mirror to really look inside myself to let go, love, and accept. In three days, all my wrenching pain was gone and has never returned.

Deep Listening

Listening with an open heart and without agenda is one of the greatest gifts we can offer someone.

By listening without judgment, you are affirming their worthiness as a person. You are holding up a mirror so they can see and hear unfamiliar parts of themselves. Listening can relieve suffering and promote peace and understanding.

Deep listening in focused presence is a healing salve for the soul—almost a spiritual experience, like meditation. I first practiced deep listening in high school when I began attending Quaker meetings in Mill Valley, California. We all meditated together in silence unless someone was moved to speak. When that happened, everyone listened deeply without comment. In Quaker meditation, you practice listening for inspiration and then follow your guidance. This experience had a profound influence on me at sixteen—and throughout my life.

It was while listening that I came to know and respect Kathleen Burgy, a spry little woman with twinkling humor and profound wisdom. When I first visited her home on Mount Tamalpais, I learned from the stories she shared that she had built it herself. She was a world traveler and artist, and she had worked for three years with displaced children after World War II in Germany and Yugoslavia. Her ability to deeply listen to me, track what I said, and reflect back to me with her own loving kindness guided my turbulent search to find myself over many decades. Thanks to her, I continue to practice deep listening with others as well as with myself.

PRACTICE: Invite a friend or family member to go for a walk or for tea. Ask how that person is doing—and be present for the answer. With sincere open questions, encourage them to share more deeply. Or make a phone call to a good friend: Sometimes it's when speaking on the phone that we get the chance to really listen. When someone is lonely, sad, or trying to make a big decision, it is a gift to track and remember what is being shared so you can be a clear mirror for them.

Find Your Spirit

One clear way of bringing deep meaning and purpose into your life is to make a connection to a source or spirit of all goodness.

PRACTICE: Have you ever felt moved by your spirit—perhaps when you see someone struggling in a precarious emotional or physical situation? If you've ever given money on impulse or offered your phone number to help, or volunteered, you have experienced the call of your spirit. Sit, close your eyes, and breathe, thinking of your breath as spirit connecting you to the light of love that dwells in everyone. Connecting to your spirit is a process, and you can find inspiration in devotions, affirmations, prayers, or music.

A belief in a Great Spirit, Higher Power, or God will provide guidance, hope, and comfort. It requires faith to believe in an unseen realm, which will in return bring you feelings of love, joy, gratitude, and acceptance.

All mindfulness meditation reminds you to be aware of your breath, the life force that animates your body and soul. *Spirit* comes from *spiritus*, which is Latin for "breath." *Inspire* means "to breathe in the life force or spirit." *Anima* is Latin for "soul" and also means "to breathe."

When I first married Gerald, he was an artist, gardener, and agnostic. I found it astounding that someone who was so loving, creative, and connected to Nature was not also convinced of a great Creator or of life after death. He had been raised by scientists and had a bright intellect that preferred proof. We held hands at every meal and said our gratitudes for one another and all of life. When I had a health scare, unbeknownst to me, Gerald wrote a prayer to God and placed it on my

garden altar asking that I be well. His prayer was answered—and without discussion, he began to believe. Months later, after his cancer diagnosis and his death, I found that hidden note. I was moved to tears. Belief in God, and that our souls continue after the death of our bodies, is a great comfort to me—and I believe it made the end of Gerald's life more meaningful as well. I was with Gerald the moment he died, and I feel privileged to have witnessed his spirit leave the body. And I continue to feel his spirit now.

Passion for Place

Tell me about the place of your childhood and I will tell you about your soul-scape, your dreams, and the seeds of your ethics.

I was a free-range child, running in the hills, playing in the creek, and being wild. In summer, I fed my body with dusty warm black-berries and fruit from an aban-doned orchard. My imagination expanded as I discovered arrow-heads and burials among shell middens of past cultures. I climbed gigantic trees and thrived in the freedom and solitude of Nature. Where you are and where you live imprint your body, mind, and soul with values and visions.

Places shape us. Your love of land connects you to everything, from seasons to migrating birds, soil to native trees, gardens to food, and to the places and way you live. You may love your place for the natural beauty, cultural diversity, or history, or perhaps for the stunning man-made structures. Architecture is the sculpture we inhabit, and it shapes our lives, views, light, and quality of life. It makes up our cultural landscape and tells the stories of past and present. Maybe your place is urban, and there are musicians on a corner, a great neighborhood eatery, and a park where you know when the trees bloom. Sharing your passion for place will educate and inspire others to notice and value what is all around you both. If they too fall in love, more people will be committed and support action to protect the unique bioregional characteristics in your community and our Earth.

PRACTICE: Make a map of your community as a way of knowing your place—showing where you live and work; how you're interconnected to water, soil, food, play, and beauty; and what is important in your day. With tracing paper overlays, make layers for watershed, farmland, built areas, and places of great beauty. Make a vision layer for what you would *like* to see: a community garden, a dog park, a bike trail, a place to gather in town with benches. Share your ideas with others and see how far you can go to affect improvements and quality of life.

Dare to Serve

In hockey, there's a play called an assist, used to create openings for players to successfully make a contribution—a score.

PRACTICE: How can you make your love visible in ways that will serve and support others? Is there a place you might enjoy volunteering—with Nature, animals, children, or the elderly? Consider contributing in an area you love, whether it's restoration and conservation or goodwill to mankind. Look up servicespace .org and Paul Hawkin's *Blessed Unrest* for community, inspiration, and action ideas.

With every assist, the entire team benefits. This discipline, or way of being, creates openings for others to come to greatness. It's an excellent way to serve others. A good spouse, parent, teacher, or mentor continually creates "assists"—possibilities for others to succeed. In the end, service is a journey inward and outward that naturally weaves meaning, rather than materialism, into life.

As a teenager, I found that service brought me purpose and joy. I volunteered with the American Friends Service Committee, and my favorite project was building thirteen houses in seven summer weeks with families and other teens. Our community, and our real work pounding nails, shaped my values and perspective.

I believe that service creates wholeness. It's a natural extension from your heart and a gesture of generosity that can regenerate hope and well-being. You may be motivated by the great needs of the world and the feeling of abundance and grace you've already received. You may be inspired by spiritual workers like Mother Teresa, who said, "We can do no great things—only small things with great love." And service doesn't have to mean helping other human beings. It can be an offering of big-picture gratitude. When you look at all you are given by Nature, you realize what a generous world we live in. My friend Duncan Berry's company, Ecosystems Services, identifies what Nature does for us and how that should be valued. Rain, wetlands, rivers, oceans, and forests all provide for us by cleaning the air, supplying water, creating habitat, making fuel and food, and doing more that we usually take for granted. It is essential to cherish the services Nature provides us and find ways to be of service to Nature.

Cultivate Sufficiency

Sufficiency is about knowing you *are* enough and you *have* enough—even as we all grow, age, and change.

When I was ten, my mom got cancer, my alcoholic dad went bankrupt, my parents separated, and our family of six kids from two to twelve years old ended up on public assistance. Two years later, during the summer after eighth grade, my mom was taken away to a state mental hospital. Throughout high school, Mom was hospitalized for cancer or mental conditions, and we all had to take care of her. Embarrassed about my family situation, I did my best to excel in other areas to make up for feeling insufficient as a person. In retrospect, I realize I began a pattern of overachievement—to "look good" and achieve perfection to cover up shame. I tried to handle the chaos with control. I didn't show my vulnerability, fearing I would fall apart or that others couldn't handle it.

Fortunately, my deep belief in God and my love of Nature and creativity held me together enough to grow up. It has been lifelong work to deeply come into my own self-worth. Sufficiency is not having "hungry ghosts" telling you to do more, be more, and buy more to look better and be better. Sufficiency is the very soil we plant our seeds in—and the belief that we can blossom with the abilities we have *today*.

PRACTICE: Make up your own affirmation to help you root to your Self and place it in a prominent place, like the bathroom mirror or above your computer. Maybe something as simple as "I love you, I believe in you" will allow you to come back to center when you feel insufficient. Saying "Thank you for . . . " and thinking of as many things as you can helps profoundly shape-shift your sense of worth. Walking in Nature, working in the garden, or arranging flowers will remind you: You are an essential part of the intricate whole.

Forgive to Live

I think about forgiveness when I'm watering the garden and suddenly little or no water comes out because there's a kink in the hose.

PRACTICE: Is there a situation or person in your life you have not forgiven? Are you carrying resentment about something within yourself? Take this opportunity to be completely honest. Write down on a piece of paper: "I don't forgive _____ because _____." Reflect on how long you have been living with anger, resentment, or negative judgment, and think about how it makes you feel. Write three benefits for holding on to the resentment exactly as you're carrying it. Maybe it's outrage or disappointment, or maybe it seems easier than dealing with the situation directly.

Now write down three positive outcomes if you forgive yourself, the other person, or the situation. Is one of these outcomes viable and possible? Open your heart and offer a prayer of release. When you are ready, light a candle and burn what you are no longer willing to hold on to. Now consider steps to make amends for something you have done, or offer forgiveness to another.

I immediately straighten it out so the hose can keep its flow. Forgiveness, to me, means taking the kinks out so there can be a clear flow or grace in our lives. When you refuse to forgive someone, the kink starts, and it's usually small at first. Forgiveness might feel too hard, or you think they don't deserve it, or maybe they've just been too hurtful. You might get accustomed to low flow, and you might not even realize that it's taking twice the effort and time. Or, worse, you forget about watering all together and just dry up. As with the hose, if you don't try to untangle the mess, the situation may never improve.

In my life, it has taken me years to forgive a few situations and people (even myself)! But once I do forgive, I realize I am able to deeply water my own seeds and grow in new ways. And that's when the garden really comes into blossom. In the end, forgiveness of others allows your own life to flow better, letting grace, love, and joy stream more freely for you.

The Way of the Lover

Love is a way of being, a gift, and a rigorous daily practice.

Love is the compass to your destiny, your belonging, and the source of your transformation. Love can ascend you to ecstasy, great happiness, and joy—and it can break your heart open as you fall to your knees shattered. But, from that dark place of anguish, love can be the light to guide you into transcendence, where you experience a far greater capacity to love again and deepen your connection and commitment to your soul purpose.

Most religions and cultures of the world believe we are on Earth to love and to create. Love connects you directly to the divine creative force and can be the greatest generator behind all your best artistic work and your deepest relationships. It is the anchor that keeps you from being overwhelmed, helping you focus and make choices that reveal your essential nature. Love is the antidote to fear. Love has a great sense of humor, which keeps it from being self-conscious and controlled.

Love of self is essential for embracing yourself and keeping your self-value and care in balance—which is completely different than self-centered inflation. And love of other, whether person, animal, or place, is a catalyst. I cherish the moment of recognition when meeting a new person, when heart sparks fly and bring a twinkle to your eyes. It can happen with a landscape, a poem, or a glance of great beauty, too: Your soul is suddenly awakened. No longer in dormancy, your seeds begin to quicken and love bursts into bloom.

Once you love, you will never go back: Your soul has come into flower. Love is the sunshine, rain, and soil that bring your heart into Full Bloom.

PRACTICE: Create a personal ceremony of love and commitment to yourself and your own loving nature. Write your own vows for what you most love and how you will cultivate your seeds of love and water them in yourself—and in others with positive actions.

The path of the

Spirit-Weaver

Integrating Mindfulness, Celebration, and Blessings into Each Day

The path of Spirit-Weaver is the golden thread connecting deeper meaning and mindfulness with fulfillment and happiness. You bring spirit into each day with personal practices, celebrations, blessings, and rituals, and you weave sacred connections with your family, friends, and communities. You celebrate the collective wisdom of all things and the beauty surrounding you. You listen and engage. You tell compelling stories to invigorate the path ahead, and you commit to sustaining human and natural communities. You release the old stories of want, greed, and waste and embrace a future where enough is just right. You practice simplicity and stewardship and observe your Sabbath. You understand that silence speaks volumes. You find inspiration in others, and then teach and lead by example. With your vision and values, you contribute your unique blend of compassion, skill, and presence of mind to heal and unify your relationships, your community, and the world. Your basket holds joy and peace and a fierce commitment so that our collective souls may be healed and blessed. When you practice Spirit-Weaver, you make gratitude and celebration a part of daily life. You begin anew each day and feel buoyant with the amount of love in your heart. Empathy and compassion for others flows naturally from you. You embrace diversity as easily as you enjoy different flowers in your garden. You see and feel connections, rather than divisions. You explore a soul life that leads you to light and mystery in others and all of life. You bow and praise the Beauty of creation. You honor and support experiences that can change lives and express gratitude for opportunities to live in Full Bloom.

Celebrate
your blessings.
Sing praises of gratitude
Your basket
overflows with gifts.
There is no room for
fear or despair.
Spirit and joy reweave the
fabric of your life.

The Importance of Activism

My mother was fond of saying, "Your actions speak louder than your words."

✿ PRACTICE: What sacred action could you take to more deeply align your passions with your beliefs? Try reading Jean Shinoda Bolen's book *Moving Toward the Millionth Circle*, which promotes women's circles as a source of inspiration, support, and sanctuary of renewal for activists. She encourages you to choose actions that are meaningful, fun, and motivated by love. What positive action can you take? Can you assemble a circle of like-minded souls who would be supportive of you and your action and have fun?

She wanted us to do the real work, not just sit around talking about it. Heart-centered activism means putting action behind your sentiments. Being aligned with your beliefs manifests itself in how you use your time, spend your dollars, raise your children, vote, or even eat. It is about "walking your talk."

Julia Butterfly Hill, Al Gore, Jane Goodall, and Gandhi are, of course, shining examples of activism. Major shifts in culture (such as civil rights, a woman's right to vote, making tuna fishing safe for dolphins) occur when visionary thinkers act on their beliefs—and inspire others to join them. I especially love it when one ordinary person takes a courageous stand and strengthens an entire movement, like Rosa Parks did on that segregated bus in 1955 or Alexandra "Alex" Scott did in 2000 with her lemonade stand.

Activism requires moving from an idea to involvement to commitment to creating a new awareness. Maybe you begin by engaging your family, friends, or church in conversation. Maybe you involve important strangers or sign petitions. It may be peace, climate change, animal rights, social and environmental justice, or health. Some people have been motivated by tragedy to become activists; others are motivated by deep love. Religious scholar Andrew Harvey speaks of something called sacred activism, when we fuse our deepest spiritual knowledge and passion with clear, wise, and courageous action in all areas of the world, moving from our inner lives to the outer good.

Becoming a Peach

In centuries past—and in the goddess tradition—white was the color of virgins and what we use for weddings, red was for childbearing and seen as a color of passion, and black signified the crone and traditionally was used for grieving.

Back then, women past their childbearing years were often seen as dry and haggard, living to their midforties. Today, we are blessed with extra decades of good health and vitality, and I feel there is a transition stage I call "becoming a Peach." We can mature into the role of wise women and retain our strong, sexy, and powerful spirits, blending passion with the golden light of wisdom.

It takes years to grow a peach tree to full fruition. The success of growing sweet, juicy peaches depends on the loving care, placement, and attention the trees are given throughout their lifetime. Peaches follow the seasonal rhythms: rest during dormancy, the great push to flower, and fruit when the petals have dropped.

A Peach usually matures in her fifties and is often bearing juicy creative fruits into her seventies, eighties, and even nineties. In your Peach years, you shift from childbearing and/or career development to birthing your *own* embodied soulfulness, from creative vision to juicy manifestation. You are acutely aware of the cycles of life and the rhythms of the Earth. You act as your own soulful gardener who knows the right timing to tend, cultivate, and prune for best harvest. "Be fruitful and multiply" is a new calling to fully blossom and bear fruit that nurtures and serves others. You trust that painful experiences have something important to contribute as well. You embrace the ephemeral as more beautiful than the permanent, the patina of age more lovely than shiny-new. You revere the stories told with lines on the face. As a Peach, you remain open-hearted because you know how to use the light for renewal.

PRACTICE: **As a Peach (or as a future Peach), ask yourself these questions: How can I best serve others with my abundance of wisdom and fruit? What comes naturally to me? What do I do well? What makes me feel juicy and alive?**

Beginning Anew

For thousands of years, cultures around the world have walked a labyrinth to begin anew on a sacred path.

🌿 **PRACTICE: Every time you breathe, you begin anew—you let go of what you've held on to, and you take in freshness. Give yourself rest, or go out in Nature and try this simple meditation. Envision an old-fashioned hourglass, and empty your thoughts and worries out like the sand. You will feel the heaviness in your chest and body trickle away when you breathe and release your thoughts this way. Empty out all those old patterns, worries, and ways of thinking that no longer serve you or your family and community. Ask yourself: In which ways would I like to begin anew? Maybe it is finding a creative outlet, expressing your spirituality, or finding a job that's not just a job but your calling. You can welcome spring into your life at any time, emerging from dormancy to blossom again.**

The labyrinth symbolizes a descent into the unknown and a return with new knowledge. By walking in silence on a path that turns and circles back on itself, it appears you are far from your goal, yet with each step you are getting closer. As in life, walking a labyrinth echoes your inner path: There are no dead ends. You can never truly get lost because you are always on *your* right path, walking at any pace.

Maybe it's time to discover a new life purpose and a new way of thinking to open up opportunities and possibilities. If you face adversity, like fierce winds against you, you can learn to tack your boat like a good sailor does. How? There is no way you can sail directly

into the wind, so you must find a new angle. You alter your direction, moving in a zigzag, so the wind will work *for* you, filling your sails and pulling you forward. Take your time and pay attention to what is going on around you. Hold your vision. To shift a disadvantage into an advantage, to begin anew, you may need to change your course by catching a fresh wind. It will invigorate your goal rather than defeat you.

Make Blessings

Blessings are like golden threads that reweave your tattered soul and connect you to the gifts all around.

Every culture in the world has some form of blessing. Perhaps it's for the feast on the table as you thank the Earth. We welcome new-borns with blessings, and call on the mother and family to hold and cherish their precious new soul. Perhaps it's a commitment ceremony for love to renew itself, or to comfort the ill with healing prayers, or to let the dying know that they will be remembered.

Once, I organized a community blessing of fifty thousand oak trees to sanctify the land and keep them from being clear-cut. A local indigenous medicine woman blessed the four sacred directions, and a Buddhist priest blessed the land and the prayer flags hanging on the trees. With music and intention, the community offered back their blessings to the trees that have blessed us for hundreds of years.

Even everyday activities invite blessings. When I was young, we always blessed each car trip, and when we heard a siren, we blessed the workers and the person who needed the help. You can bless each new day with your intention and gratitude—and it will shift your perspective when something doesn't go as you had hoped for. Blessings bring a clear new perspective and awareness into your life in times of joy and abundance, as well as when you are ravished by loss and tragedy. The expression "It may be a blessing in disguise" helps you look for the silver lining. Be patient and know: *Everything will be all right in the end, and if it's not all right, then it's not yet the end!*

PRACTICE: Keep a blessings journal—page after page of blessings you've experienced or offered over many years. Some years, you'll fill pages; other years, you may not feel as blessed, but it will increase your awareness of the smallest blessing—enough rain, a year of good health, a freezer full of home-made soup. Begin to compose your own blessing for the day, a loved one, or a special event. Offer it to your family and community. My favorite inspiration is John O'Donohue's book *To Bless the Space Between Us.*

Create Celebration and Rituals

I used to always push myself from one great project to the next, barely stopping when something was completed.

PRACTICE: Select a date for a celebration—to honor a small feat with a simple raised-glass toast or celebrate a milestone with a special meal and a wide circle of participants. Honor the little steps and the milestones as you accomplish goals in your life and as you and your family and friends pass through the many happy and sad passages of life. It will nurture you along your path.

My list of what needed to be done was never-ending, so I just went on to the next task. I finally realized that not only was this exhausting, it wasn't any fun either. It was a form of self-denial that led me to overwork, stress, and depletion.

What I needed was a celebration. Celebrations bring joy to life— and a welcome pause to acknowledge a milestone or accomplishment. Creating celebratory occasions weaves friends, family, and community together with food, conversation, contemplation, laughter, and sometimes even traditional music, dance, and dress. When you celebrate your important life moments, it gives others an opportunity to witness your accomplishments, which is inspiring both to them and to you.

Celebrations are also a joyous way of commemorating people's lives and remembering them with love after they have died. I've helped create many ceremonies to honor deceased loved ones with blessings, flowers, poetry, music, food, and photographs. We often decorate an altar with flowers to symbolize ephemeral life and beauty and with candles to symbolize our eternal inner light. Depending on the tradition, there can be a very specific ritual: prayer, music, or the ringing of bells to awaken your life calling. Rituals have deep meaning and can contribute to a significant emotional, spiritual, and legal impact on your life (think about marriage or baptizing a baby in a Christian church). Burial rituals have been performed for tens of thousands of years. And rites of passage are celebrated throughout the world for certain age groups. Rituals help families and their community pay homage to someone's life and bring blessings, healing, tradition, and closure.

Find Compassion for Yourself

Compassion is the twin of empathy. It is your willingness to see through the eyes of another, allowing your heart to feel their pain, challenge, and loss.

I worked for years to feel compassion for my mother. She was sick with cancer and mental and emotional issues for half my life and died on my twenty-first birthday. She had wonderful qualities I appreciate and emulate to this day, yet she also had very challenging and deeply hurtful behaviors that caused much pain and damage. For me to transform my suffering into compassion required soul reparation, and I needed compassion for myself first. Like making a garden on an old city lot, there was a lot of my *own* debris to clean up, deep digging to do, and new soil to be brought in. Only then could I root and flourish. I had to forgive myself before I could sincerely feel compassion for my mother. It provided emotional strength—and resilience.

There is no better way to transform old patterns of judgment than to put yourself fully into someone else's position. It nourishes generosity and kindness, which in turn reduces anxiety, strengthens personal relationships, and increases self-worth. From scientific studies, we know that the hormone oxytocin, also called the love hormone, is released when we feel acceptance, love, belonging, and connection. Having compassion brings a soothing peace and contentment to your heart.

PRACTICE: Try this simple, comforting meditation: Take your left hand and place it over your heart. Take your right hand and place it over your left hand. Now breathe, closing your eyes. Picture a person who unconditionally loves you—this could even be a religious figure. Breathe in the love anchored in your body, feeling trust, safety, and complete acceptance. When you are ready, give yourself a hug and open your eyes.

Then sit down and write yourself a letter from a place of deep understanding and acceptance: "Dear darling precious, I see you. I love you. I appreciate you. I understand the pain of your losses and disappointments. I know how difficult it was for you. I so appreciate your loving and open heart. I will always be here for you." Sign it and mail it to yourself to read later.

Of Death and Impermanence

Death has been one of my greatest teachers, defining my life and stretching my ability to be present in the midst of loss and brokenness, even though it's one of the hardest lessons in life.

PRACTICE: Close your eyes, imagine your heart, and see any little cracks. Picture love coming down like liquid gold, pouring from the heavens, to fill your heart, making it stronger and more beautiful with radiance. Imagine the flowering of all the love you have cultivated in your life blooming in your heart. Breathe into that.

To acknowledge impermanence, cut hearts out of paper, punch a small hole in the top, and loop ribbon through. Then write words, quotes, or poems about love on each heart and hang them in your garden. As they blow in the wind, they will wear away over time. They will bring both blessings and a reminder of impermanence of the object and the memory.

Whether it's a person, beloved pet, or a beautiful tree, a permanent loss reminds us of our own mortality. When a person has suffered, death sometimes holds a quality of relief. Other times, it's shocking, and we become angry at the injustice of it. When death can be full of love and support, and when we can guide the dying into their next life with breath, love, and comfort, it becomes a chance to grow and reflect.

I cared for my sister-in-law, Pam, every other week. We sipped and savored life, leaning inward, embracing all goodness and joy. We toasted small moments—like Pam having enough energy to get out of her pajamas and ride in her wheelchair like the Queen Mother, wind blowing in her wig, her one-year-old daughter holding her hand. Her death was peaceful, at home, circled by family and flowers and angelic music. We breathed her last breath together. We dressed her in the lace dress she had chosen. At only thirty-six, Pammy's body was done, ravished by cancer.

A couple of years later when my great love, Gerald, was diagnosed with brain cancer, we both thought this was only a test. After brutal treatments, he died five months later. His strong body and brilliant mind resembled someone in his nineties, not early fifties. He died in the emergency room, with me holding on to his feet as I expressed my love for him and my willingness to let go as doctors tried to restart his heart. I brought his body home for a gathering of friends and family. Letting go was the hardest task of my life. My heart was broken.

It was when I could visualize his love like liquid gold filling my

The temple bell stops but I still hear the sound coming out of the flowers.

—Matsuo Basho

heart that I realized my heart's capacity had expanded and I was healing. Recently, when the time came for my seventeen-year-old dog, Toolie, to die, I was prepared but still devastated. Letting go of what you love because of death is one of life's most challenging experiences we all face.

In Buddhism, one of the holy truths is to acknowledge impermanence in life as you practice complete presence in the moment. They teach that letting go of attachment relieves suffering. I think that is true, but I have work to do because I am still very attached to what I love.

Listen to Your Dreams

Some people believe night dreams can be important messages from your higher Self or source.

🌿 **PRACTICE:** Do some seeding of your nighttime dreams by asking for a dream you'll remember in the morning. Then, when you wake up, tend your dream by writing it down—whether it's a snippet or an entire "movie." The more you practice, the more you will recall important parts of your dreams. Record how the dream made you feel in your body and what you thought about when your eyes opened. As you journal your dreams for a few weeks or months, you will begin to get insights into symbolism that may inform your life.

Nighttime dreams provide hints and insights from the unconscious, unrestrained side of you that is wild and open. Through images, symbols, and stories, you are given pictures of delight, mystery, or fright. Keeping a dream journal will help you remember, track, and interpret them. On the other hand, daydreams connect you to your imagination, inspirations, and aspirations—and open you to new possibilities in your daily life. It is often in stillness or a meditative movement like yoga when our bodies are occupied and our minds can wander and dip into other realms.

Community dreams bring new visions that inspire and lead society into new directions. Just think about Dr. Martin Luther King's speeches and the thousands of people who were brought into a new field of consciousness. A dreamer sees and feels something first—and then articulates that vision and inspires a shift that others can follow. There are dream cultures, like the Achuar people, that plan their day according to the message or vision from their dreams.

One of the gifts of my mother's long illness was her doctor Jamshid Bakhtiar, a Persian Jungian psychiatrist with a heart of gold. His kindness and deep knowledge of dreams was a guiding light. He transformed my mother's suffering to a sense of peace before she died at forty-seven and guided our family to meaning and purpose by interpreting our challenges as the archetypal hero's journey, giving each of us a new dream.

"Yes, I am a dreamer, for a dreamer is the one who can find his way in moonlight and see the dawn before the rest of the world." —Henry David Thoreau

The Joy of Giving

All religions of the world promote generosity.

Buddhists believe that it is one of the Ten Perfections and the antidote to the self-poison of greed. Islam teaches generosity to please God. Christ taught his followers to serve and share resources. Those of the Jewish faith tithe 10 percent of their income to support charity. Indigenous potlatch feasts, with enormous giveaways, were an early traditional gesture of philanthropy and redistribution of wealth—a status symbol of how much you could give your guests. The Scottish Enlightenment philosophers proposed that to be enlightened, the essential key is happiness obtained by practicing a kind of "fitness" exercise of self-development. One must do good deeds to help others and live within your means in harmony and balance with Nature.

Generosity is an act of kindness that generates more love, goodwill, and well-being for others, benefiting both the giver and the receiver. *Philanthropy* is a love of humanity—nurturing, caring for, cultivating, and enhancing what it is to be human, whether it's culture, arts, public good, or the environment. Both generosity and philanthropy can be accomplished through donations of your time, money, things, or skills, as you volunteer or provide goodness and beauty to others. Perhaps you share your books with a free mailbox library at your house, or you share your love of literature by teaching someone to read. Giving food and flowers, or listening to someone in need, are all gestures of generosity. Time and money can be viewed as energy, and to keep us healthy, that energy must be circulated like water and not be allowed to sit and stagnate. Generosity is an antidote to hoarding and a testimonial to trusting abundance.

PRACTICE: We come from a most generous and generative Earth and universe. What have you received and how has the generosity made you flourish? What and who are you grateful for? Identify the generosity that's come in small and big ways, whether it was advice, unconditional love, financial assistance, or something tangible or intangible. Then consider which of your generous acts have given you the most joy? As you share your time, wisdom, and resources, you'll discover that generosity regenerates you.

Know Your Happiness

We *all* want to be happy and in a state of joy and well-being.

PRACTICE: Make your own map to joy: Write the word *happiness* in the middle of a large piece of paper. Write what and who makes you happy and why, branching out from the center. List people, places, creative activities, food, spirituality, music, beauty, holding a baby or an animal, reading poetry, attending a funny film, or exercise. How do these things connect? Keep coming back to your map and add to it with insights, a collage, or drawings. Naming your happiness can be as much a spiritual practice as an insight into your lived values, like taking an environmental inventory of your life.

Fortunately, this generous emotion is sowed as freely as wildflower seeds into the hearts of our friends, families, communities, and the world. We just need to water it with our thoughts and actions. Philosophers, religious leaders, psychologists, and even economists have studied what makes a person and society happy. Scientists tell us that being happy is 50 percent genetic, 10 percent environmental, and 40 percent how you see the world. The lesson? We have a lot of freedom to choose our point of view. Sometimes it takes an experience, a teacher, or a practice to inspire you to reflect on your life and shift toward more purpose and meaning, as Scrooge did in Dickens's *A Christmas Carol*.

Spirit-Weavers know what makes them happy, and, in turn, they create happiness for others—not as an obligation, like a codependent and never-ending job, but with their authentic presence. My friend's husband nicknamed her Tinker Bell because she sprinkles fairy dust of joy and playful exuberance wherever she goes and still provides

depth and meaningful rituals, ceremonies, and celebrations for everyone lucky enough to know her. Whenever I ask my friend and spiritual seeker David how he is, his consistent answer is, "I'm in bliss!" He recognizes his blessings and expresses his sense of great joy. We may see people doing backbreaking labor or living in great poverty yet they are very happy. It's in the way they see the world.

Five Universal Forces

Five universal forces are recognized in most cultures of the world.

I learned to integrate these forces as practices from Angeles Arrien, a cultural anthropologist. Perhaps there are some you do each day, while others may be harder. There's no order, and none is more important than the other.

Heal. Embrace healing each day. It always occurs in a natural rhythm, medium to slow, never in the fast lane. High trust needs rest. We each carry our own unique medicine, and it is our honor and duty to develop it and share in the world. I feel an urgency for each of us to step up and offer our healing gifts.

Initiate. We can initiate or ignite the spark of learning something new every day through observation, curiosity, and open-mindedness. An initiation is often marked with a rite-of-passage ceremony, celebrating the acceptance or entrance into a group when people have demonstrated they have learned something well enough to be included into it.

Create. Create something new every day with intention. It could be music, art, writing, or food, or in a garden you tend. Creating might emanate from a child you nurture, a story you tell, or how you dress or set the table with flowers and color. Bring your innate creative force to play each day.

Integrate. After reflection and contemplation, this force unifies separate ideas, deepens them, and makes sense of them. It intermixes people, concepts, and beliefs and makes them whole, balancing fragmented parts in yourself or community.

Transform. This is when you come into your own, unfolding or blossoming. It ensures you will grow or change through big insights, life crises, or transitions. Like a turn of the seasons, your old references and patterns transform with a new inner knowing that you integrate into your behavior and your actions.

PRACTICE: Track in your journal how you have integrated each of the five universal forces each day. Which is more prevalent in your life? Which takes more effort? Which has the most meaning? If we want to integrate a new behavior, it requires a daily practice of twenty-eight days, so try tracking one force for a week, then adding from there.

The Healing Power of Humor

Humor allows truth in through the back door, inviting in a new perspective.

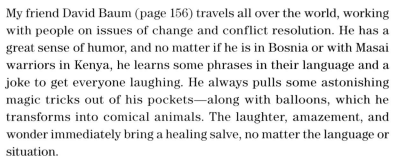

🌿 PRACTICE: Cultivate your own sense of humor, and learn to laugh and make others laugh. Listen to comedians or humorous storytellers. Learn to laugh at yourself, to stay humble and authentic as a way to stretch and become more flexible. You might learn to tell a good joke or tell a funny story. My friend Sandy has a quick, joyous wit—and her dad, a dentist, always kept a notebook in his shirt pocket full of good jokes he'd collected. Try doing the same.

My friend David Baum (page 156) travels all over the world, working with people on issues of change and conflict resolution. He has a great sense of humor, and no matter if he is in Bosnia or with Masai warriors in Kenya, he learns some phrases in their language and a joke to get everyone laughing. He always pulls some astonishing magic tricks out of his pockets—along with balloons, which he transforms into comical animals. The laughter, amazement, and wonder immediately bring a healing salve, no matter the language or situation.

I like that humor, humility, humus, and human are all related. I think being a gardener and working with humus keeps you humble—with a sense of humor. I would always choose humor over a sword to transform situations and open hearts. Invisible, yet powerful, humor can transform a group and bring laughter, weaving disparate individuals together. When you can laugh at yourself or your situation, you loosen your grip on your attachment, revealing your flexibility.

Although there are culturally different kinds of humor, laughter is universal. The word *humor* actually came from the Latin *humor*, meaning "body fluids." Laughter releases our body fluids, and has been recognized since ancient Greece as a way to improve mental, emotional, and physical health. Humor reinvigorates you and replenishes your spirit.

Trust Your Intuition

Intuition is your inner voice, gut feeling, or hunch.

When you cultivate your intuition, it becomes your compass, providing a guiding tool to navigate your right path. It can become a shortcut you recognize immediately—feeling it in your bones—before you think consciously or reason something out. It can be your personal North Star on an uncharted life path. And it becomes stronger and clearer as you begin to trust and follow it—like having more lucid dreams when you begin to write them down and honor them. As with any skill, practice listening to and following your intuition to improve your ability to see it. It will lead you to your calling.

Historically, intuition has been considered communication from the Divine, Higher Self, or Higher Power. Serendipity, those happy beneficial "accidents" or unexpected pleasant circumstances, seems to come to us more when we are following guidance and in the flow with the Mystery. These surprises become affirmations and encouragement from the Universe—or God. Yes, *you* are on the right path and *you* are being guided and watched out for.

I used to get confused between my intuitive guidance and voices of guilt, control, or insufficiency. I had a strong critic that pushed me into overdrive and perfection. If you have a similar voice, don't feed it with your time and attention. Rather, cultivate a voice of clarity and support, which is usually simple and direct: "I can trust this person." "Don't go to that party." "Take more time to make your decision." Practice listening and following, and experiment with paying attention to how it feels in your body.

When I silence outside voices, noise, and distractions, I can settle into the gift of my intuition—like drinking from a clear, deep spring of knowing.

PRACTICE: Set aside time in silence, perhaps when doing meditative work like gardening or walking, to listen to your own deep knowing. I sometimes even speak out loud to hear a new idea. Write down the pros and cons of a situation—or person—and then tune in to your body and listen to your gut. You might even get digestion problems if you can't "stomach" something—or, like me, get a backache when I have overdone my commitments and need to "back out" of something. Begin to track what happens when you follow your instincts.

Leadership

Though there are many different kinds of leaders, strong ones always have clear vision and integrity, which ignites the imagination and hearts of others as they show the way.

PRACTICE: I have noticed that most inspiring leaders have a spiritual core they turn to for guidance, and they move with authenticity, not arrogance. What leaders inspire you? Track their visions, character qualities, and how they attracted followers. What can you learn from them and their charisma, communication skills, and collaborations? Find and read Godin's book *Tribes: We Need You to Lead Us.*

As gifted communicators, charismatic leaders weave hopeful messages with stories that unite and inspire their followers to greatness. Good leaders listen keenly and respond to others with empowerment that recognizes the skills of others to trust and collaborate together.

These days, there is a need for diverse leaders from a full spectrum of race, gender, economics, age, place, and style. Developing skills of listening and openness to many points of view are important for all of us. We can all learn from different cultures how leaders are chosen or formed. For some people and situations, walking shoulder-to-shoulder in conversation works better to build relationships, while others may prefer a circle for dialogues. Some might plan a round of golf to foster camaraderie; others work together, with everyone contributing their skills. Joanna Macy, born in 1929, is an eco-philosopher, environmental activist, Buddhist scholar, ecologist, and visionary leader for what she terms "the great turning" back to compassion and care of the Earth. At 83, Barbara Marx Hubbard is a futurist, a leader in coevolution, and expert on conscious evolution. Both of these women have the gentleness of a grandmother and the strength, clarity, and fierceness of a samurai. We need leaders like them to inspire people to fall in love with beauty, Nature, spirit, and one another so much that we each recommit to all the work and changes necessary to be healthy and wholly functional on Earth.

Garden artist Monet was a leader, too, because he followed his own light for guidance—and his approach to beauty with clear vision, hard work, tenacity, and values inspired generations. To develop leadership skills and a clear voice, you must respond to your own spirit and your highest calling with commitment.

Following the Light

When I lived in an eighteenth-century barn in the village of Varengeville-sur-Mer along the Normandy coast in France, I spent my days following the light.

I lived close to the elements and became completely in tune with the place. The light would wake me up and whisper to me where to photograph that dawn. *Go into the wild woodland. Today, visit the rose garden. Look for fairies by the old espaliered apple lattice in the potager.* I would follow swiftly on foot with my tripod and camera, quietly arriving where I was instructed. Each time, I would be awed. Sometimes I was moved to tears by the beauty—and I would say a prayer of gratitude, promising if I was allowed to photograph such light, I would share my photographs to open the hearts of others. At times, I felt perhaps I had spent too much time alone noticing every nuance of light, but then I realized that this is what Monet had spent his *entire life* doing.

For me, it is Nature's gift to illuminate our own divine spark. After all, life itself is literally and metaphorically dependent on light to grow. As Gardeners and Artists, we recognize the breathtaking beauty of light coming through a leaf or bringing sparkle to a dewdrop in the early morning apricot light. When light is especially beautiful, I feel surrounded by grace. Light is also a direct reminder of the sacred or divine spirit around us all the time. Sometimes we meet people who "light up the room," and we can feel that light shine from within them.

PRACTICE: Create a ritual to celebrate light (the summer solstice and winter solstice are great occasions). Rise with the sun and open your heart to all that it lights up. Notice the colors come alive. During the day, observe the changing of the light, and in the evening take time to watch the sunset, noticing again the warmth of the afterglow. Wait for darkness to come, and look for the moon and stars. Then light just one candle to witness how much brightness it brings to the dark. Meditate on your own light, how you keep it burning, and how much brightness you bring.

Open to Being the Lotus

When the light is right, the lotus ascends through the water, emerging into full bloom.

PRACTICE: How do you handle the mud in your life? What conditions do you need to rise to the top and bloom? Try this: Plant an indoor bulb like an amaryllis or a paperwhite and watch its growth over time. Affirm to yourself each day: "Today I stretch down my roots into the rich darkness, trusting I have all I need to bloom. I will gradually seek the light, emerging and unfolding to my own fullness."

The lotus is like a large water lily planted underwater in the mud. In Asia, Egypt, and Greece, it is a spiritual symbol of awakening and enlightenment. Anaïs Nin, the American author who journaled her entire life, reflected on the time in her life when it was less painful to bloom than to remain tight in a bud. To unfold and find your heart center, you'll need to be courageous.

It isn't easy. Once, I was in a stuck-in-the-mud relationship, not ready to emerge and fully bloom. I lacked the confidence to grow into my own power, beauty, and largesse. We married because I thought that would bring the commitment and depth I sought. He did not welcome our pregnancy, and, to my great devastation, I delivered a premature stillborn child. In the following days, I imagined laying on the ground and being covered by the Earth; as a gardener, the thought felt comforting. Concerned my image was too much like death, I changed my vision to instead see myself walking in a garden with flowers much taller than me: blue delphiniums, pink foxgloves, red poppies, and tall yellow hollyhocks. I decided to leave the relationship in order to bloom.

That is when I emerged from the mud, and my life began to flower! I moved to a house by the sea in Carmel and had a nurturing relationship with a gardener who filled my home with flowers, music, and joy. Later, I traveled to Europe and fell in love with Monet's gardens, quit my job, and moved there. Less than three years from my devastating miscarriage and failed marriage, like a lotus I was walking among towering flowers like those in my healing vision.

Meditation and Prayer

Meditation is a time to simply let go of thoughts and focus your awareness.

Some people memorize and repeat a word or inspirational phrase, while a visual person might benefit from seeing an image in their mind's eye. The image could be a deity, a mandala, or a flower.

Whether you meditate in silence, with music, alone, or with others, you connect with a precious moment in time. With my friends Duncan and Melany Berry, I meditate on the phone with them once a week after a brief sharing of our lives. To begin, one of us rings a bell, and we share ten to twenty silent minutes together coming into our breath. We end by ringing a bell and often share an inspirational reading. It is very dear and nurturing to share this time together, even though we are apart.

Prayer is powerful in silence or spoken aloud, sung, read, memorized, or repeated. Prayer can also be spontaneous utterances like "thank you," "help," and "I love you." Movement like yoga or dance can be offered as a prayer, and prayers can enter into weaving and beadwork, connecting each bead or thread with the Divine. You can offer prayers of praise and gratitude and petition for blessings, guidance, or healing. Prayers, both formal and spontaneous, are a meaningful way to commemorate life's thresholds like births, marriage, illnesses, and death.

I believe in the power of prayer, and I say prayers throughout the day. Prayer for me is a conversation with God. Asking for help in times of stress, challenge, or heartbreak helps me feel supported to stretch myself and not break. Prayers of thanks bring appreciation, and daily practice brings comfort and familiarity.

PRACTICE: Begin a simple practice of daily meditation or prayer. Sit still in a comfortable place, close your eyes, take notice of your breath, and bring your thoughts into your body. You might imagine a rosebud opening, petal by petal, into full bloom; this is who you are right now. Offer a prayer above you, behind you, below you, and all around you. Feel it go into your heart and carry it with you throughout your day.

Find a Mentor

Having a wise person in your life who truly sees you and wants the best for you can help you realize who you really are.

PRACTICE: If you've never had a mentor, find one for yourself. Your mentor can be a paid professional—like a great teacher, a skilled coach, or a trusted therapist—or a wise friend, colleague, or elder who can help you realize your true potential, without having a personal agenda. With mutual respect, your mentor may support, guide, witness, and track your growth as you strengthen your voice, discern your calling, and live your life on purpose. And when you feel ready, be a mentor to a youth, sharing your wisdom and life resources.

With the guidance of a mentor, you may recognize yourself in a way you never had the courage to see before. A mentor helps you hold your gifts and tap into your inner resources, so you can move out of fear to step into your soul's calling and figure out which path to take. A mentor invites you to show up in your full strength and beauty to express your truth with a wide-open, strong, clear heart. Your mentor can be the plumb bob, knowing where your center point is—and as a clear mirror will show you your current self and encourage you to realize all of your growth potential.

My life has been blessed and guided by numerous mentors at different ages and stages of my life, and I, in turn, am honored to have been sought out as a mentor to many youth and people in transition. Mentoring is a sacred relationship of great respect, intimacy, and love. A mentor must be trustworthy with good boundaries and self-discipline. I think it is important to believe in each other and be clear and steady within yourself. My mentors have been patient gardeners, helping me to cultivate my skills, distinguish what needs pruning, and feed my soul with loving nourishment.

Presence of Mind

Mindfulness goes hand in hand with presence.

You can't have one without the other, and they are linked together in a life-giving way. Being present, aware, and conscious allows you to savor life to the fullest. The simplest way to be mindful? Connect to your body with conscious breath. It's like your own mini spa time for personal relaxation.

Of course, mindfulness requires focused discipline. Many athletes are deeply absorbed and present in their body, breath, and environment when they catch a wave, hit a home run, or sail in high winds. Nature, too, can call you back to the present when a wave hits you walking on the beach, or a loud bird swoops down and cries out, or you come upon deer grazing in a meadow. These moments of awe and wonder, when we see beauty, give us presence of mind.

So does great joy and loss. As a culture, when we are sad or grieving, we want to fix it and get over the pain as quickly as possible. But I have found that if you can fully stay *with* your sadness or grief—accepting it like a garden in winter, tending it with kindness, patience, and faith—it will transform. Pruning, weeding, and turning the soil with composted suffering will bring the new growth and light you desire.

Mindfulness brings clarity and depth because you empty out the clutter of the mind. It's like working in a clean kitchen or on a clear desk: You know where everything is, and there is a sense of spaciousness. There's no panic or confusion. Clarity invites spontaneity, humor, and ease. It is an opportunity to empty out and reconnect to body—to refresh and begin anew. Experienced meditators transform their suffering and bloom into love and compassion.

PRACTICE: Many people don't feel they have time to meditate even though they know it is good for them, but a little goes a long way. Begin a daily two-minute practice breathing with conscious awareness. Do it while taking a shower, washing dishes, walking, or waiting for something, then gradually increase your time with joy.

The Big Picture

When astronauts looked back to Earth when *Apollo 8* went to the moon in 1969, the image of our planet floating in the black sky had a life-changing effect on the world.

PRACTICE: **Has "getting there" or getting it done ever been so much your focus that you forgot to look back and get perspective on your actual experience and how far you have come? Reflect on your life journey. What does the overview of your life mean to you? Go to www.vimeo .com and watch the short, powerful film called *Overview*. Feel for yourself the awe and wonder of seeing Earth from afar, and appreciate how fragile and precious our planet is in the cosmos. Decide which three personal actions you can take to support the vital health of Earth.**

Getting to the moon had been the focus, and no one realized that those breathtaking photos would create a new kind of self-awareness across all of humankind. We felt a profound sense of connectedness with a full understanding of our fragile and precious ecosystem. To see Earth just hanging in space became the most important gift of the trip.

As the astronauts floated out of their seats, they were overwhelmed by the beauty of such a dynamic, alive place—the spectacular colors, the line of day and night moving across the globe, shooting stars, storms, and the fireworks of the northern lights. Astronaut Edgar Mitchell recalled realizing that we are all stardust, and all life comes from the same organic sources. Author Frank White coined this transformational perspective the Big Picture or "overview effect." The astronauts witnessed, from a cosmic perspective, that the sun is a star in an ever-expanding cosmos of one hundred billion interconnected galaxies and the immense rareness of Earth.

Author and futurist Buckminster Fuller was correct: We do live on "Spaceship Earth," a living, breathing organism with a paper-thin sky. We are not separate from Nature; we are a part of, not apart from, the whole.

Observe Your Sabbath

Traditionally, the Sabbath is a day of rest, a time to reconnect to the sacred in your life and give thanks.

You may attend church on Sunday or temple on Saturday, or spend time in Nature as your renewal. It's a day of the week you can give yourself to unplug from your work and daily routines—perhaps even disconnect from computers, phones, and televisions. You have a chance to slow your pace, enjoy family time or alone time, work in the garden, walk in Nature, read, write, reflect, or cook a slow meal and eat it with gratitude.

I have spent many years in France, and I love their long lunches, leisurely dinners, and four-week summer vacations—all part of their norm. It provides a wonderful quality of life and rhythm: It strengthens families and allows time for preparing delicious food that everyone shares around the table. It encourages well-being and creativity. In an article in *Sierra* magazine years ago, I read about studies of this enviable French lifestyle, with statistics on how much better it was for not just them but the environment as well. They used far fewer natural resources, and their population's health and happiness were far better than the average American's. We work forty hours or more a week, only take one to two weeks off a year, and have soaring health problems from stress, backaches, and depression. No wonder the French have the wonderful expression *joie de vivre*—the joy of living. Let them be our example.

PRACTICE: Choose a day for your own Sabbath to rest and connect to beauty and your own spirit. You might choose an hour each day or a few minutes throughout your day for a Sabbath. I have friends who set bells on their computer or phone to randomly go off so they will stop and breathe consciously. Take a nap or sleep in; it's the best and simplest thing you can do for your health! Find your own joie de vivre. Choose a staycation, enjoying your home and community. Maybe you'll take a break from a consumer-based culture, choosing a simpler life or moving toward a life that's more sacred.

The Sound of Silence

I grew up visiting nuns who had taken a vow of silence, and I could not imagine what their lives were like.

🌿 PRACTICE: **Give yourself the gift of silence. Unplug your electronics, phone, TV, radio, computer, and recorded music. Finding this stillness in the midst of your busy life will guide you to your "formable middle," a place from which you navigate. Some people sit in silence. Others discover that meditative actions like yoga, swimming, walking in Nature, or gardening fills their wells. Find what nurtures you.**

Years later, a wealthy society woman and mother of six I knew amazed everyone by joining that same silent order. She was ready for a life of contemplation and simplicity. Twenty years ago, my mentor, Kathleen Burgy, invited me on a silent retreat weekend led by Thomas Moore, author of *Care of the Soul*. I was delighted but worried how I would manage in silence for more than a few hours. I found that the quiet and the intentional silence in community nurtured me in a way I never imagined possible. It was profound.

Since then, I have spent many days alone in Nature slowing down, going inward, resting, deeply integrating, and emerging with a clearer authentic voice. Being in tune with the rhythms and sounds of Nature and witnessing the changing sky, moon, and stars have helped me root deeply and blossom more fully. I've led and been a part of retreats where we share meals, walk, work in the kitchen, and garden in silence—not talking from dinner until after breakfast. I am amazed at how nurturing it is and how you can deepen relationships without talking.

There is a kind of silence that is nurturing, full, and abundant—nothing like the empty, hollow silence of loneliness that can drive you to despair. This silence invites you into an inner stillness to get beyond distractions, pain, and sadness. Finding that silence will refill your well, which gets depleted from periods of emotional drought and overgiving. Silence quiets your busy mind and relaxes your nervous system. It is crucial for self-reflection and inner soul connection.

A Gift to Be Simple

Simplicity means being natural and easy to understand.

It's beautiful when you clear away the unnecessary adornment, decoration, or pretense—like in Shaker furniture or Japanese gardens and architecture. It can be a good design solution (look at Apple). It takes work to edit, but being able to explain something complex demonstrates a depth and clarity of understanding. Simplicity is often associated with truth—the simplest theory is usually the most truthful.

Some people practice voluntary simplicity as a spiritual practice. They focus on things that are important to them—like living in balance with the Earth and developing their character and spirituality. When you simplify your life, you have more energy, time, and money to pursue what you love and believe in.

I have sung the words "'Tis a gift to be simple, 'tis a gift to be free" most of my life and believe that it is far more satisfying to live simply with love and delight than aim for great accoutrements and trappings of wealth. Simplicity is often a choice, and today it can seem a radical one against the marketing norm. I appreciate elegant simplicity as an aesthetic and all things handmade. Simple food gathered from the garden or the farmers' market, prepared with laughter and friends and served outside on a table full of flowers, is more fun to me than a fancy dinner.

Being content with who you are is the essence of simplicity. It will satisfy and quiet the mind that says—thanks to the brilliant marketers who have tried to make you believe this—that you are not enough and that you need more stuff. When you know who you are and what little you need, your life becomes enriched with abundant time, generosity, and joy.

PRACTICE: **When has simplicity enriched you? Where are places in your own life you could simplify and gain more time and space? Whether it's your schedule, your closet, your desk, or how you cook or garden, it can probably be simplified to gain more time, beauty, or relaxation. Even cleaning out a drawer can bring clarity and simplicity. Look at the video *The Story of Stuff* on YouTube and the Web site www.storyofstuff .org for more insights. Practice saying, "What I have is enough!"**

Stewardship

Stewardship is the act and process of being responsible caretakers and recipients of the place you live.

It flows both ways: You are stewarded by where you live, the water that nourishes and cleans you, the Earth you walk on and that feeds you, the air you breathe. Most cultures and religions teach the environmental ethic of "care of creation" and care of Nature, as well as stewarding your personal resources of time, talents, health, and wealth.

My friend Kay Cline, a retired schoolteacher, heads a sustainability group to restore parks in her town that have fallen into disrepair due to lack of funding. With musicians playing lively music, community volunteers work joyfully, cleaning and planting neighborhood parks, reweaving community and relationships. Kay and her partner, Bill, have spent countless hours with many others to create a new vision for the stewardship of open land that was once Fort Ord. This has required collecting thousands of signatures, going to city and county council meetings, going door to door talking with neighbors, and setting up a table at public gatherings to have conversations. Part of her discussion is to envision ways to steward this land, the water resources, and open space. As a result of local efforts, in April 2012 President Obama signed 7,200 acres of the land as Fort Ord National Monument. That size will double when it is cleaned up.

Two friends of mine, Paola Berthoin and Marie Butcher, partnered to inspire the community to become stewards of our local watershed and Carmel Valley River. It is their heartfelt work to reconnect, reimagine, regenerate, and restore communities, culture, and habitats.

PRACTICE: Ask yourself: Do my work, my actions, and my lifestyle support life? In what ways am I stewarded by the place I live—and how do I reciprocate? Find ways to steward that which is nourishing and stewarding you, whether it is relationships, land, historic buildings, public parks, plants, finances, organizations, or political processes.

From Deep within Your Soul

As a Spirit-Weaver, you develop a relationship with your soul by listening to your intuition and tuning in to your destiny.

Whether you're young, old, or middle-age, male or female, you can develop a compass, unique to you, to navigate your choices and align your path. Time in silence, in meditation, in contemplation, or in prayer will open and deepen your communication with your kind of divine guidance. Some people may employ ancient tools of divination—like the Chinese *I Ching*, tarot cards, a pendulum, or astrology—to be guideposts and provide insights. Others may pay attention to their night dreams and derive insights and messages from their unconscious. Time spent reflecting in Nature will always nourish you. With practice, you will know in your body and heart what is true.

I learned a skill from philosopher and author Jean Houston that helped me become more aware of and familiar with my Higher Self as a resource for guidance on my path. Here's how it works: Try using your imagination to conjure up an "Old Friend" who has always known you, loved you, and accepted you just as you are—from before you were born to after you die. This friendly soul has your personality, humor, and passions along with the wisdom you would have if you'd lived a thousand years. This friend could be your guardian angel, your beloved teacher, your guide, or your Higher Self, who has complete faith in you and the long-range perspective of knowing you *always*. Her clear, strong love and belief in you nudges you to your greatest potential and belief in yourself, giving you courage and confidence. Call on this Old Friend anytime to stand with you; she or he is your constant companion.

PRACTICE: Feel the complete love and acceptance of your Old Friend, releasing any judgment you may have of not being good enough. Breathe into that love. Feel your own love and self-acceptance *right now,* right as you are. Now close your eyes for at least a minute and think of something that made you really happy: time with a dear friend, your wedding day, making something beautiful. Accessing joy opens your heart and puts your mind in a flow state of happiness, trust, and receptivity. Spend some time in Nature or a quiet place with your journal. Write in your journal, as a dialog with your Old Friend or Higher Self, asking for clear insights. Try writing a question with your dominant hand, then allow a response to come through while writing with your nondominant hand. This process accesses the more creative right hemisphere of our brains, and you are bound to get a fresher, uncensored response.

Find Your Tribe

It is a wonderful feeling to find your tribe—a community of friends and family members with whom you resonate.

PRACTICE: Call up a couple of your friends and invite them to walk or have tea and suggest giving mutual support by listening to ideas, sharing new creations, and having meaningful collaboration and fun together. You might like to read religious scholar and poet John O'Donohue's book *Anam Cara: A Book of Celtic Wisdom*. It means "soul friend" and will assist in your quest for deep friendship and meaningful support. Consider areas of your life you would like to have more support in—your love life, family, art, finances, health. What are you currently being challenged in and in which areas would you like support in order to take a risk and truly blossom?

A solo instrument is spontaneous and wonderful—but an orchestra brings an incomparable diversity of complex depth and resonance.

You are related in love, shared passions, support, and stewarding one another. You play, create, and collaborate, committed to being there for each other. You are related by choice, bringing out the best in each other and yourself, accepting and forgiving any shortcomings. Each person feels safe to be authentic, which promotes true creativity and risk taking. Growth is cultivated; goals are supported and celebrated. Your life is rich as you reweave the basket of community that holds all your joys and sorrows, hopes and dreams. Feelings of loneliness and isolation—which often lead to depression, overconsumption, and addictions—are resolved. Tribes inspire generosity. They are greater than the sum of their parts. Small intentional acts of kindness and compassion add up faster and with more joy.

I love volunteering in residential work camps. No matter where or who we are, we always form our own tribe. One of my favorite life experiences was spending seven weeks building thirteen houses in the scorching San Joaquin Valley in California, with a dozen teens and the Chicano families who would live there. We invented a new culture of optimism and fun as we went. Our recreation was swimming in the irrigation canal and making a gigantic seesaw from two extra roof joists. We lived in two houses with concrete floors and open stud walls, with black tar paper and chicken wire wrapping the outside. We took turns cooking simple food that we blessed while holding hands, and ate together around a plywood-and-sawhorse table. Our wealth was singing, playing the guitar, and laughing. We were empowered by real work and camaraderie, forming amazing bonds with diverse ages, races, and economic backgrounds. It taught me that tribes include and never exclude.

My artist friend Jo Anderson is part of a tribe called the Bear Sisters, who meet once a week to drum, journey, and create together. They have met for *twenty years*. Friends can be a tribe of joy and celebration—as well as being available for the difficult times of illness, death, and loss. They share their deepest callings, finding resonance with one another, weaving their loving support by offering courage, food, help, and collaboration. They bring out the best possibilities in each other, supporting and bringing one another's dreams to reality.

We used to show our strength and independence by doing everything alone, being self-sufficient, and not asking for help. Now we realize that collaboration and mutual support for one another's visions, work, health, and well-being help us thrive and contribute to the world.

"There is almost a sensual longing for communion with others who have a large vision. The immense fulfillment of the friendship between those engaged in furthering the evolution of consciousness has a quality impossible to describe."
—Pierre Teilhard de Chardin

All Kinds of Time

Time is both a mystery of our human life and something we measure.

We keep track of it with clocks and calendars in a consistent manner, but time is not equal. There are good times that fly by and bad times that drag on. There are times that you will always remember and times you hope to forget. There is the first time and the last time. There is a moment when time stands still in shock, joy, or pain. There is the big question of the time after death: What is eternity? Whether you believe in the eternal soul, life after death, or even multiple lives, what we know for sure is *this moment* is only once.

Some very busy people wake up and already feel they are running late and don't have enough time, while others have "time on their hands." They have time affluence—yet they don't realize how wealthy they are. Most of us want *more* time, but we can't buy it. When I teach, I try to give the feeling of having "all the time in the world," a sense of timelessness that happens when you do art, listen to music, dance, or watch great theater. You get lost in reverie—and time seems to stretch; timelessness invites creative flow.

Many children and teens rush to have adult experiences, while adults often reflect on their childhoods and how they were raised, what they did, and how thoughts shaped them their entire lives. A split second can change everything in a life that has had consistent rhythm and routine for decades. Time spent in solitude and contemplation can enrich your soul, or it can feel even more isolating. Time can become more meaningful and precious to people in confinement from illness or injury or even prison. Programs of art, meditation, and creative writing can allow their lives to blossom. In the garden, all of time surrounds you. It takes time to grow a plant. The soil is made of dinosaurs and meteorites so ancient we can hardly comprehend it. Water and air unite us all, while old trees carry the history and story of hundreds of years ago to the present living moment.

PRACTICE: Give yourself a day to slow down. Stretch your time—be present, sip, taste, enjoy, and savor. Like a child with a precious piece of candy, suck on it slowly to make it last, get out all the flavor, and experience the senses. Put a single raisin in your mouth and eat it as slowly as possible, noticing all its textures and sweetness. Dine slowly, exercise slowly, walk slowly, make love slowly.

Following Your Calling

Vocation comes from *vocare*—"to call," to hear your calling, your life's work, your soul purpose on Earth.

It is more than just a job: When aligned with your heart, your work becomes your offering, your contribution, and your prayer. Some people have a career that is also their calling, like teaching, medicine, art, or being a monastic. Your vocation may evolve in response to what the world needs and as your own development emerges.

Vocation also comes from *vox*, or "voice." You must listen for your deeper wisdom as your intuition and develop your clear outer voice in the world. Most children sing freely, dance, paint, and draw with heartfelt abandon; later, many lose their confidence to express themselves individually. No wonder so many adults find themselves in unhappy jobs that don't align with their calling and values.

As a young child in a Catholic family, it was recognized that I had a calling, and I was encouraged to be a nun. At nine, when I was taught by a nun, I realized the convent was not my calling. I considered being a doctor, but I fainted at the sight of blood. As a teen, I began a spiritual search, checking out different beliefs, practices, and religions. By my early thirties, as an artist, gardener, author, and world traveler, I had suffered some traumatic losses of marriages, children, and family members. I told my beloved mentor, "I am going to become a Jungian therapist, like you!" In the kindest, wisest way, she said, "Lizzie, precious, you would be a very good therapist . . . but there are already many very good therapists. You have something special that you must discover—follow that." She saw me in a different calling, believed in me, and encouraged me to continue on to find, create, and follow my own authentic life.

PRACTICE: In your journal, reflect on your life as if from your deathbed. What are you happiest about? What do you feel are your greatest accomplishments? Who have you loved and who has loved you? Are there any regrets? Is there anything missing you wish you could have done? What do you want to be remembered for? Write that down and reflect on it. A life review is an ancient way to get to the core of your life while you are healthy, like a good gardener reflects on which seeds to water and which to weed. Take steps toward finding and following your calling.

Wisdom Keepers

Wisdom Keepers have wide-open hearts full of love, compassion, and empathy despite having experienced brokenness.

🌿 PRACTICE: Who have been your wise teachers? Did you have an elder, friend, or teacher who saw you for all your worth? How did they encourage you, offer advice, and move you along? Write them each a thank-you note, telling them how their wisdom enriched your life. How can you, in turn, use the qualities of a Wisdom Keeper to inspire peace and loving kindness around you? Collect or write stories, poems, and songs from your own culture, and share the wisdom with others through storytelling. Perhaps you have a story from your own life or a classical one. Tell it!

Are you a Wisdom Keeper? You may hold the insight of your family and your culture—and have the ability to integrate and transform bitter experiences into clear guidance. Maybe you've been nurtured by wise elders, grandparents, teachers, or neighbors who have seen and recognized you. You may have witnessed profound wisdom coming from a youth or child full of innocence, optimism, and fresh perspective.

Wisdom Keepers hold a basket of healing antidotes that they have gleaned from their life experiences and grown into good judgment and a broad body of knowledge. They hold the qualities of being good listeners, and they are patient and kind. Traditionally, Wisdom Keepers hold vision and offer guidance for their community. Some can offer at least one hundred healing stories, one hundred songs, and one hundred poems—dispensed like medicine with the right dose and prescription for each situation.

Wisdom is to be shared, sometimes as a beacon of light, sometimes as a mirror, and sometimes by simply being present. The greatest wisdom is being able to hold your worthiness and to transform your self-doubt into self-trust. They know how to heal themselves and offer healing to others. If a branch breaks in a storm, the tree can still repair, regenerate, and come back into blossom and fruit. Wise people know how to take pain and loss and shift them into something that supports growth. They know the rhythms of life and essential practice of replanting what doesn't come up the first time. They know how to till the soil of their hearts and souls, because without the opening, there will be no place to plant, and grace—like water—will not be able to soak in.

Zen Sticky Notes

My Buddhist friend Duncan Berry calls his handwritten *gathas* "Zen sticky notes."

They're little spiritual reminders to get him back to his center point when he gets off balance. A gatha is a Sanskrit term meaning "verse" or "hymn." Duncan has filled a small notebook with them, and he refers back to it like a personal prayer book. He has written his most potent reminders on sticky notes and has them stuck to his computer and bathroom mirror.

EMBRACE
Patina of Age.
Spirit shines
through You!
TRUST YOUR
HEART!
FULL BLOOM!

Now I have Zen sticky notes, too, and they're tucked in my wallet, my car, and my bathroom kit when traveling. For me, they are simple cues, like little candles illuminating my path when I lose myself. Shorter and more personal than most prayers, they blend positive visualization statements and personal haiku that hold my intention. I also make them for friends and leave them in their house or car. Once, I had a major meltdown when I thought I had lost all the digital photographs from my computer and had a deadline for a major show at New York Botanical Garden. I was beside myself. I lost all my perspective and went into complete insufficiency—a messy, dark spiral. Duncan suggested I write some of my own gathas to help lead me back to my centered, capable self. I found it helped me transform my anger and halt the feeling of being overwhelmed. After about two weeks, I was able to find the photographs, to my great relief and appreciation. Here is one I came up with:

PRACTICE: Create your own personal gathas, mindfulness prayers for some area of your life where you need support and strength. Write them on sticky notes, or jot them down in your journal for easy reference. You might even write some with your family or friends for encouragement and as an affirmation of your feelings for one another.

MY COMPUTER

I am grateful for magic.
Mysterious web
connects me to world.
I smile with inhale,
flowers bloom in my heart.

Beautiful images emerge,
I exhale. Happy.
I play with light, joy!
I create order, peace!
I breathe.
Happiness.

FULL BLOOMERS

Full Bloomers live a braided life, weaving all four pathways into a life of meaning, action, and gratitude. These Bloomers featured in the pages ahead are my personal friends, and I love and admire them. Together we have worked, played, prayed, and created *rituals*. Discover how they have explored and developed qualities found in the four pathways and why they have integrated the practices into their lives of purpose and *service*. These Full Bloomers have explored their unique passions and contributed their *creative* skills to make the world a better place. Each Bloomer weaves community with family, Nature, creativity and *love* and then shares blessings through celebrations, ceremonies, and rituals. These stories will inspire you to follow your intuition, create right livelihood and happiness, and live with purpose and joy.

Betty Peck,

a dear friend, mentor, and inspirator, is the very definition of Full Bloom. She saturates every part of her life with gardens, art, love, and ceremony. And, at ninety-two, she still lives by a creed—the child in the garden and the garden in the child—that has been not only the foundation of her fifty years in the classroom, but a guiding principle in the relationships she fosters all around her. When she created the ten-acre Saratoga Community Garden in 1972 with Allen Chadwick, it was an idea far ahead of its time, and some six thousand children a year visited until it closed in 1987. When she built her own garden (in the Silicon Valley) with

her beloved husband, Willys, she chose everything, from playhouses to rain barrels, with young eyes in mind. In an area renowned for cutting-edge technological innovation, Betty consistently reminds us that children need time in Nature to root them in the values of the Earth. It seems that everything Betty ever started is "in" again—the importance of play, imagination, experiential learning, children being in nature, and organic gardens—but her own convictions have never changed. "I consider every day precious, and count any day a child is not in the garden, one lost," she says. "Every day in the garden is a celebration."

And she's known it all along. Betty was offered her first teaching job before she graduated from college at San Jose State—the old California State Normal School— taking the helm of a third-grade class of fifty-plus students at University Avenue School in Los Gatos. After she was hired to be a supervisor of K through third grades, she realized that Kindergarten was where it all began and started teaching it in Saratoga a short time later. With it came the first line of her Kindergarten teacher's creed: "I bring the gift of myself to this celebration of life we call Kindergarten." And she made each and every child feel loved and grateful for the very same gift. "If a child forgot how wonderful he was, I would bring him in and open the magic cupboard door, and I would put my hand on his shoulder," she says. "I would say, 'look at yourself!'" Around the full-length mirror was written in calligraphy, "Thank you for every magic moment that makes it possible for me to stand here and feel how truly wonderful I am."

In the early 1970s, a principal of a nearby elementary school asked Betty to start a new Kindergarten program. She told them she wouldn't accept unless she had a class-

room oven for baking bread and a door straight into a garden. "I wish that every Kindergarten door would open onto a garden to really learn what the world is all about," she says. "We were designed to be in the garden. Children need time for gathering wisdom—with no words, because words get in the way. Once the wisdom is gathered,

Discovering the Oneness of All Life in the Garden

the words will have meaning." Betty believes that the wisdom of the world is to be found in the garden: cultivating, planting, tending, and harvesting.

You only have to step into her extraordinary heritage garden in Saratoga to see how credo takes shape. What a garden it is! Entering it, through an arched gateway covered with fragrant honeysuckle, is like discovering a secret that holds unknown adventures. Betty believes that the need to "enter into" establishes a separation between what is and what could be, and creates boundaries—a beginning, an ending, a permission to begin anew. The sense of anticipation and discovery inherent in a garden's yearly cycle mirrors the cycle of life, and this connects each child to his own life's rhythms. Her Kindergarten vegetable garden has winding paths for processions and are lined with fragrant plants like lavender and mint, to connect children to the source of their food. Tree stumps are just twelve inches high so children can sit and look right into the faces of flowers—their "golden center," as Betty calls it—which allows them to feel their relatedness to Earth.

In fact, almost everything in her gardens is placed with enrichment, merriment, and growth in mind. Under a canopy of blooming trees, there is a sandbox made from branches and filled with shells. "The building and rebuilding of everything that has been a part of their lives is a vital part of the sand play," she says. "Re-creating the world is the work of childhood." Willys Peck—a lawyer, historian, editor, punster, poet, and printer—loved trains, and he built his own narrow-gauge railroad to give rides around the property to children. A beautiful throne, made of bent willows, is where Betty

gathers the young and old around her for songs and stories. The compost bin for the school is located in a place of honor, and every leaf of the deciduous trees and every rabbit dropping is claimed to place here; during the spring, it is distributed with great ceremony, showing children how life turns to death and death into life.

The couple's son, Bill, and Willys, both Shakespearean scholars, constructed an outdoor amphitheater called the Theater on the Ground; the community comes with potluck lunches or suppers to sit on benches beneath towering oak trees and watch performances. Betty also has a delightful little garden house, and inside there are only books about gardens—and a big comfy chair from her Kindergarten classroom days with an appliquéd woman sitting on it, called the Mother's Lap. Someone who is feeling sad or needs to curl up in comfort can snuggle into the Mother's Lap, look into the garden through the vine-covered windows, pull out a gardening book, and just read.

But the garden is not just for young people. Overlooking the creek below, comfortable armchairs sit around an old gypsy wagon used as a table. Painted on the back of a bench: "Cultural Change Through Conversation." This is where friends gather every Thursday, at her salons, to exchange ideas to help heal the world. It even gave rise to one of her books, *A Kindergarten Teacher Looks at the Word GOD: Reflections on Goodness, Oneness and Diversity.* For Betty Peck, it is through deep listening and openness to diversity that we can bring about peace, respect, and understanding. With her daughter, Anna Rainville, herself a teacher, musician, and community weaver, Betty teaches educators, doctors, and parents—*us*—that the integration of all learning is rooted in the garden: mathematics, science, storytelling, cooking, social graces, art, music, singing. She teaches us that regular patterns—like weekly garden chores, phases of the moon, and seasons—help us develop and recognize our own personal rhythms, which anchor us in the cosmic passing of time.

I first met Betty at a retreat for women writers led by Dr. Clarissa Pinkola Estés on a cold California coastal weekend in January 1991. When thirty women were asked to introduce themselves, Betty and I were the only ones who proudly said we were writers and gardeners. From the first, there was a spark of recognition between us. Later, on the way to lunch, I caught up with her. She was wearing earthy-green linen knickers, patterned stockings, rather worn pointed gold shoes, and an embroidered peasant blouse, and her long white hair flowed down her back. (I soon discovered this was her signature artist-of-life costume.) I learned that she is a cultivator of beauty, a risk taker, community weaver, master Kindergarten teacher, magic maker, mythologist, mother, and wife—an authentic, one-of-a-kind self.

But more treasured than all of this, for me, is Betty herself: Her capacity to recognize people enables them to feel celebrated and honored, no matter who they are. I soon discovered, too, how everyday rites are intensely important to her. One of Betty's most treasured habits was to make afternoon tea and take a walk around the garden with Willys, her cherished life partner. They'd stop to sit in a double sliding rocker and admire the view of the creek, and count their blessings—*every day*. "Willys understood that the vibration of life's functions must be met, the rhythmical getting up at the same time each morning," she says. "Four is tea every day, Monday is yoga, Thursday is salon, Sunday we read the *New York Times* and the *San Jose Mercury News*. Willys never has an unkind word. His favorite saying is, 'Yes, dear.'"

When his health began to fail, his family kept a loving watch over him in their home. Friends brought flowers and food, played violins, and engaged in conversations of wit and depth. Salon met, but the rhythms of life slowed and quieted as when snow falls—but the blanket that enfolded them all was the warmth of love. When Willys passed away in April 2013, the entire village honored him in the very church where he had been baptized eighty-nine years before. The Pecks' renowned hospitality, generosity, and gifts from their hearts

have deepened all who know them. Their life together was a path of love, and their home and garden deeply reflect their dual passions.

For more than fifty years, Betty and family have continued to celebrate May Day together with their children, friends, and students in an open, sunny spot called The Golden Ring. One lucky year, I was honored to be the May Day Queen, welcoming the dancers and asking the piper and young violinists to begin. Betty presided in her spring-green dress, adorned with ribbons and rosebuds; we all wore flower

crowns made from vines in the garden. She serves her traditional strawberry shortcake with cream from the last real home dairy in her area. This past year, as we wove the green and yellow ribbons into a braid on the maypole, we celebrated the great spirit of Willys and Betty and the way they have woven their community together. Life into death, death into life.

The Pecks' garden still enriches all the senses, as any garden does: hearing birds as they splash in a bath, smelling the perfume of baby roses, petting a bunny, and nibbling wild strawberries. At play in the garden, each child discovers the secret of life. There is always an opportunity to develop a relationship not only to the Earth but to the whole cosmos, coming into contact with the literal and metaphorical mystery of life. Betty is still connected to her own childlike wonder. In fact, the first time she found her calling in the world, she was just a young girl of twelve. It was during the Depression, and she and her family had moved from near Los Angeles to her father's ranch in Modesto, California. Her mother, a city girl who said she "would try this for the summer," found that the farmhouse was too small for her six children. She asked the men to bring up the big hay wagons, piled high with thick bales. "There, beds were made with sheets and blankets stacked to the sky," says Betty. "Unbelievable!" She and her siblings slept together under the black night, with meteors racing across their dark outdoor ceiling. "At that moment," she says, "I was caught up and became one with the universe. I wish that for every child."

The Kindergarten Teacher's Creed

I bring the gift of myself
To this celebration of life
We call the Kindergarten.

I come each day
To be refined, smoothed, tempered,
For I hold in my hands, with wonder and gratitude
The future!

Seeds of the future are in the oneness
Of all nature and all people
In tune with the divine to be found in our hearts
That I give, through the joy and beauty of love.

—Betty Peck

Lita Judge

There was a time when Lita Judge—who went on dinosaur digs at just fourteen years old and studied to be a geologist in college—never imagined she'd become a full-time writer and illustrator. But one night after dinner, as she and her husband, Dave, were washing the dishes, she told him for the hundredth time: "If I could do anything in the world, I would love to write and illustrate children's books." Instead of just nodding passively like usual, he threw the dish towel down and said, "Just do it."

She began working on her first book the next day.

While following her passion was a risk, Lita's tremendous commitment to her creative process and her love of Nature have always been her life path. She and her twin sister were born on a little island in the Alaskan wilderness; their nearest neighbors lived in a rustic Tlinkit village and they took floatplanes to the mainland. Their parents were wildlife photographers, so her entire childhood was spent observing Nature all over the remote backcountry of the West. As her parents photographed grizzly bears, watched cubs play in the snow, encountered moose, and followed tracks, Lita made sketches of animals in her little notebook. But the love of animals didn't stop at her parents: In summers, Lita's family visited their grandparents, who were respected ornithologists—complete with a Wisconsin farmhouse menagerie of owls, hawks, and eagles. "We rose before dawn to study hawks in the wetlands," Lita says. "And my grandmother shared a strong bond with a golden eagle. Each spring she would bring the eagle sticks, and together they'd build a nest. Her observation was so keen that it seemed like they could talk."

These moments weren't lost on young Lita, who spent hours watching birds and drawing what she saw, developing a patience, tenacity, and sense of adventure that has stayed with her ever since. In fact, she met Dave in college and became friends when they took a bicycle trip across the country with a group—three thousand miles, thirty days, and only ten dollars per day for food. After everyone else in the group dropped out, the pair kept going. They had to travel light, carrying no more

than thirty pounds, so they ended up with just one spoon for eating. But they knew that when the going got tough, they could make it. There was no calling home for support; it was up to them. "All you need in life is a good creative challenge," she says, along with clear focus and a strong goal. By the end of the journey, Lita and Dave knew they had a rock-solid commitment to one another and would spend their lives together. "We pedal at the same speed," she says.

Choosing Happiness, Creating Joy

They returned to finish college, living in a funky (and leaky) trailer next to Forest Service land, sleeping under the stars, and eating lots of potatoes to save money. Lita made note cards and sold paintings—and over one million bookmarks—at outdoor shows. Whenever the two of them earned some extra money, they'd take off for Europe to get inspired by the places, the art, and the artists there. Lita carefully sketched the architectural details and captured the spirit of each wonderful place, and when she returned home, she created large paintings fresh with the beauty and joy she'd just seen. In time, she was able to quit her job as a geologist and make art full-time—and became an award-winning author, sharing her great love of animals, painting, and telling stories to bring children closer to Nature.

Today, Lita and Dave live in a big red farmhouse they built in the woods outside Peterborough, New Hampshire. Every detail is lovingly considered in the architectural features, collections, and colors of their home. No plain white walls here: There are beautiful greens, oranges, and golds. Decorative shelves hold select treasures. This magical space was inspired by her grandmother's farmhouse and the home of Swedish artist Carl Larsson, whose home was near where she studied and worked. Their property is wild enough that bobcats, bear, deer, and fox walk by the windows of her studio— and Lita can quickly sketch their gestures. She has made woodcarvings of ravens inspired by the Pacific Northwest indigenous art. Her studio looks like a barn from the outside and a church from the inside, with a giant Gothic window that she found and salvaged. Details were inspired by a church she and Dave visited in Ireland. "I painted

in the kitchen of a small house for years, so when I finally built my studio, I dreamed big!" she says.

Everywhere she turns, Lita finds inspiration, especially from watching and drawing animals. The Judges' two cats and a little parrot named Beatrix (after her hero, Beatrix Potter) are muses and companions, sitting on her shoulders (yes, one of the cats does this, too!) and making her giggle. The time she spent with her grandmother—and now with Beatrix—stirred her to write *Bird Talk*. When Puma, one of her cats, looked quizzically around a corner at her one day, she started drawing a grizzly bear with twinkly eyes looking around a corner with a similar curious expression—and he became the main character in *Red Sled*.

The ideas are all around her. "I write in my journal and draw almost every day, and I need to draw for an hour to become fluid, like an opera singer warming up her voice," she says. "Then I'm in a zonelike meditation, and I work from my imagination. Usually it's a visual idea that comes first to me for a book. A character pops into my imagination and begins to talk to me, asking for a story." But some tales, like *Pennies for Elephants*, are true—it's about children in the city of Boston who collected money, one coin at a time, to save elephants from the local circus. *One Thousand Tracings* celebrates Lita's mother, who, as a little girl, collected clothes and food for people in Europe after World War II.

Because she's recently had to manage chronic pain and difficult medical treatments, the past few years have presented some extraordinary challenges for Lita, but her pluck, creative spirit, and love of life keep her going. After a hiatus, she began small paintings on eggs. At times, her hands were too weak to hold them, and they would drop—shattering hours of work. A friend brought her gourds to paint instead. But now her favorite thing in the studio is a birch tree draped in white lights and covered with 150 blown eggs whimsically decorated. To strengthen her hands, she worked with clay and, rolling it into coils over hundreds of hours of physical determination, constructed beautiful pots and urns, and another new art form developed in her life. With her patience and clear intention, Lita has gotten strong enough to paint again, with a less taxing and simpler illustration style that's infused with even greater joy. In spite of her obstacles, she continues to create incredible delight for children and adults alike. "I get up every day and know I choose to be happy," she says. "It is my responsibility to be happy, to keep my commitment to my passion, to set goals, and to celebrate beauty and animals."

By following her continual curiosity, remaining positive, and pushing beyond all of her setbacks, Lita has developed wonderful new talents, finding gladness and healing with her creativity. Through everything, Dave has always had faith in what Lita needed as an artist and has always been the silent partner supporting her passionate and creative life. The two of them talk about her ideas every morning at breakfast. While Lita is in her studio, Dave—a computer genius—updates Lita's Web site and creates films about her. His quiet, independent nature allows him to pursue his own work and, at the same time, give Lita the time and space she needs to create. I'm so inspired by Dave and Lita's commitment to one another, by their lifestyle of simplicity and beauty, by the way they bring artistic spirit to their daily lives. As Dave told her once, "I believe you are the best investment we could make."

> **"It is my responsibility to be happy,
> to keep my commitment to my passion,
> to set goals, and to
> celebrate beauty and animals."**
> —Lita Judge

David Baum and Terry Reeves

No matter what time David Baum comes home to the small town of Peterborough, New Hampshire, from his international travels—whether it's working with a Fortune 500 company or leading a retreat in the deep wilderness of Kenya or northeastern Canada—he goes out with a flashlight to check his plants. He's grounded and renewed by the rhythms of the garden and nurtured by its beauty and growth. The wonderful 230-year-old house where he lives with his wife, Terry Reeves, a former Outward Bound instructor, is surrounded by flowering perennials, sacred space, and Nature. Over the years, the two of them have created and planted beautifully textured perennial borders around old stone foundations and ancient trees. It's a sanctuary for all who visit, whether from across the field or around the world.

And visit they do! Once, it was ten Tibetan monks who stayed for two weeks while they practiced the sacred art of sandpainting and led meditation at the Mariposa Museum, where Terry works. Another time, a dozen inner-city youth from artist Lily Yeh's Village of Arts and Humanities in Philadelphia came up to dance during the Children and the Arts Festival that Terry organizes every year. Native American elders have stayed to offer sweat lodges, rituals, and blessings. Visiting artists give workshops and lectures. The couple's generosity is more than food and a bed: Their guests come right through the kitchen door and become family, welcomed into their lives, their town, and their activities, enriching the entire community.

David does peace work with people in the midst of great change or in the throes of recovering from war or trauma, whether it's the government of Northern Ireland, the Temagami First Nation, or Survivor Corps. He has one doctorate in

organizational psychology and another in divinity. He's written the insightful and humorous *Lightning in a Bottle: Proven Lessons for Leading Change*. He was even a clown in the circus—he can juggle or breathe fire, and he uses his magic tricks to amaze, delight, and educate the people he works with. I think his magic tricks are so good he could do a show in Vegas, today. He's a great conversationalist. I love David's sense of humor, a quick wit that both ignites and unites others. He brings his brightness and spirit to every

Weaving Community with Magic, Humor, Creativity, and Inspiration

encounter—conversing about post-conflict Bosnia and Herzegovina or Rwanda, walking the ancient path of the Prophet Abraham in eastern Turkey side by side with regional leaders, meeting with philanthropists, or simply listening deeply to Terry.

And Terry is the grounding rod: She literally keeps the home fires burning to prevent the pipes from freezing in snowstorms while David is out in the world. The Mariposa Museum focuses on multiculturalism, respect, and the understanding of diversity—in a real sense, teaching peace with the folk art in its collection. Terry designs an educational curriculum for the museum that brings children and community to work with guest artists from around the world. For years, she has worked as an artist in the schools, teaching children how to make handmade pop-up books and enormous papier-mâché puppets for Peterborough's annual Children and the Arts Festival. Conceived over twenty years ago, this all-day event closes the town's streets and fills the community with song, laughter, puppets, costumes, music, and creative chaos. Terry and her team of merrymakers work with kids of every grade and school to make puppets with a theme: One year it was Peace, and after studying Gandhi and his nonviolent practices, they built a ten-foot puppet of the leader. Hundreds of colorful prayer flags were made in the park and hung all around town, bringing with them both art and cultural awareness.

Terry is a wonderful artist and a natural teacher, and she's extremely organized—instead of a family room in their home, they have an art room, with many shelves and labeled boxes full of art supplies and how-to books. It's a magnet for creativity, and it's such a dream room for me that Terry helped me make one in my own home.

I met David almost twenty years ago in the desert, on a twelve-day vision quest with cultural anthropologist Angeles Arrien, and over the years we did several more together. There's a comfort in being alone, fasting, and immersing yourself into spiritual reflection in the serenity of the desert, with plants that teach adaptations and a sky that invites you to know the cosmos. It connected us with depth and respect. I've become a frequent family member in their home, and I've witnessed how David and Terry's love of Nature, creativity, and diverse cultures makes them citizens of the world, informing their values and giving them the fluency to drop into dif-

ferent environments and be with people intimately and respectfully.

And I've witnessed their love for each other. One of the many things I admire about Terry and David is how strong and how important their marriage is—and it's a second marriage for both of them. Terry had two young children when they first met, and David has been an active and committed stepfather to Kate and Galen, who are now young adults. Thanks to in-depth work with Dr. Arrien, they practice being very clear in their communication: When there is a disagreement, they set aside time to talk about it and resolve it, but not without expressing their love and gratitude toward each other. Their dedication to one another is clearly stronger than any upset or anger. I have great admiration for how they coparent in a blended family, respecting the needs of the children and their biological father, and for the loving mentorship David has given the children.

He has been a wonderful example to them. Kate and Galen are both spending

several years in Kenya, working with the largest youth-helping-youth organization in the world, Free the Children, which David counsels. They lead projects building schools in Maasai villages. In the Me to We program—which transforms people into world changers one action, big or small, at a time—they teach American and Canadian youth to think as a community while they experience Maasai tribal life. They inspire youth to think as a global village, to emphasize in a bigger connection of all people. It's all about making better choices, about "walking softly, traveling lightly, and making a difference." After graduating

from college, Kate and Galen, both wonderful artists who know and love Nature, have developed into international leaders dedicated to service.

When David was sixteen years old, his father, just forty-eight, stepped off the court after a doubles tennis match and died in his arms. It shaped David's life from that day forward. When he was in his midforties, one of his personal ambitions was to hike Machu Picchu, the sacred site in Peru. After training for a year and traveling for more than twenty-four hours, he and Terry arrived in Lima—five thousand feet in elevation. All of a sudden, his chest started sending sharp pain throughout his body. Thank God there was a cardiologist at their hotel, who told him to return home immediately. They took the next plane back to New Hampshire, where David had his biggest heart-opening experience yet: quintuple bypass surgery. David provided recordings of Coleman Barks reading Rumi poems to hear while he was under anesthesia, as well as have the surgical staff listen to. Many friends prayed and drummed for him, as the drum is used cross-culturally for connection to the heart, love, and healing. And David healed remarkably well.

To celebrate life and express their gratitude, David and Terry hosted a creativity weekend around his birthday, inviting many of their most creative friends from near and far. We flew in from France, Ireland, Canada, and across the United States. David carefully orchestrated our time together with meaningful conversations, rejuvenating walks in the garden and Nature, and shared food and song. Terry and I made an altar and decorated tables with the abundance of New England's autumn. We gathered for a blessing and dinner together in a huge tent in the garden on Friday. On Saturday night, on the top of their property, we participated in a traditional sweat lodge ceremony led by a medicine woman, Virginia McKenzie, from the Temagami First Nation. In the dark, we spoke from our hearts as water poured over the red-hot volcanic rocks. The spiritually renewing ceremony of purification grounded us to Earth in harmony and respect. It was more than just a fun weekend away: We got to know one another with intentionality and depth.

Terry and David hosted this event annually for five years, and they continue to use their property to weave together their spiritual beliefs. Mirth and magic intertwine their lives. And David? He has since returned to Peru and hiked the famous Inca Trail to Machu Picchu, becoming an inspirational poster child for his regional heart hospital. He continues to shepherd change with his particular flair for the delightful. David has found his art as a passionate gardener, where change is a part of each day. Looking forward to the unexpected, he practices his Tibetan overtone chanting and centering rituals, and together with Terry, they cultivate their soil and the soul of the Peterborough community. Whether it's personal or natural, for circles near or far, I find it a miracle such beautiful regrowth comes up after devastating winters and challenging times.

Melany and Duncan Berry

When Melany Berry met her husband, Duncan, more than forty years ago, she was an enthusiastic, Nature-loving teenager working at a YMCA camp called Westwind on the wild seacoast of Oregon. Duncan was a commercial salmon fisherman and younger than she. The land and the ocean made a big impression on both of them: The ever-changing river and its beaches are animated by drifting fog, veiled woodlands, bluffs, and swaying Sitka spruce trees. The tidal river ebbs and flows, making silver brushstrokes in black sandbars. When Melany was introduced to Duncan's father, he taught her meditation through breath and the Heart Sutra, and though it took her a long time to figure out exactly what it meant, she knew that this practice—along with a reverence for land and sea—would play a central role in her life.

Duncan and Melany married a few years later. They both are wholeheartedly engaged in "right livelihood," the fifth step of the eightfold path in Buddhist teachings. This step advises us to earn our living in such a way as to entail no evil consequences, to seek employment to which we can give our complete enthusiasm and devotion. Not

that it was easy: Duncan, a talented artist and entrepreneur, went from being a fisherman to a jeweler to a T-shirt designer, which ultimately led him to found Apparel Source, Inc., a large clothing company. But in the 1990s, he realized the extent of the environmental damage—through pesticides and synthetic fertilizers—the cotton industry was causing.

It was then that Melany asked Duncan, "What do you want your lasting impact to be?" The answer was clear: creating healthy habitats and humans through business activities. Though becoming an environmental steward wasn't simple or straightforward, Duncan was resolute. When he discovered that buying organic yarns was prohibitively expensive, he hired an agronomist to work with farmers in Pakistan to grow their own organic cotton. His new company, Greensource, and their partners in Pakistan provided financial assistance to those farmers in seasons when cotton wasn't being grown so they wouldn't use pesticides to grow other crops. They funded seed banks, well digging, and even an elementary school for 150 children in Vinder, an Arabian Sea town. Greensource became the first company to market sustainable fiber products to the mass market, and it wasn't long before it was providing organic cotton for Walmart's baby clothes, sheets, towels, and yoga wear. Duncan became a visionary leader in the organic

Creative Stewards
of Land Heart and Sea

cotton movement, and it's just one example of his whole-systems thinking and commitment.

But what truly mattered to both Duncan and Melany, what they were ardent about, was the land and environment around them. They worked for six years to save a 13½-acre estuary on Vashon Island, Washington, called Fern Cove Sanctuary, preserving a small jewel of natural forest and tidelands for the Puget Sound community where they were living and raising their family. Later, in 2006, they sold their visionary Greensource to create and endow the nonprofit Westwind Stewardship Group, which acquired their beloved Westwind's 529 acres of pristine shoreline. These days, Westwind provides transformational and educational experiences in a magical place of land, sea, for-

est, dunes, and estuary for five thousand summer campers, families, and retreat goers annually. The Berrys are now able to mentor new environmental stewards every day. "But stewardship flows both ways," Melany says. "Walking the Earth's surface can heal and nourish us in times of trial. Its water feeds, cleans, and supports every form of growth in our lives. We need to fiercely steward that which is nourishing and stewarding us, whether it be relationships, land, plants, finances, organizations, or the political process."

In fact, *steward* comes from the Old English word for "house guardian." So it makes sense that Westwind is where the Berrys have made their home. Their cozy house sits like a mothership above the grounds, with a commanding view of Cascade Head and the Salmon River Estuary. The nine thousand acres surrounding them has been designated a United Nations Biosphere Reserve. It's so valued for its extraordinary biology that it doesn't belong to a state or even a country, but to the whole world.

It beckons exploration, and I've been lucky to explore with them many times. I met Melany more than twenty years ago at Esalen in Big Sur while attending an Angeles Arrien retreat, but I genuinely fell in love with Westwind and the Berry clan when she invited me to attended the Great Turning, a New Year's celebration based on the work of eco-philosopher Joanna Macy, PhD, in 2001. At dawn, Duncan led Buddhist meditation and mindfulness, then yoga, for anyone who cared to join. We participated in multigenerational conversations between the "earlies, middles, and elders," with everyone sharing their feelings and insights on questions about work, food, and love. Melany, who's also an internationally trained chef, planned all the meals using local, organic, and seasonal food. Bonny, Duncan's sister, made her famous cinnamon rolls, pies baked with wild blackberries she'd picked during the summer, and homemade granola—pure delight. Kaj Wyn Berry, Duncan's mother, created calligraphed banners with inspirational quotes and hundreds of WindWishes—blessings we put in the trees to send our wishes and dreams out with the Pacific Northwest winds. Their grown children—Alalia, a doctor, and Morgan, a welder and artist—were there helping out, too. We cooked local organic food with Melany in the happiest kitchen I had ever been in. We

gathered driftwood for big bonfires, everyone bundled shoulder to shoulder in freezing weather, happily playing music and singing together. We made beeswax sand candles and paper lanterns for New Year's Eve, and all seventy-five of us sang in a procession down to the river with little boats made from found natural materials. In each, we placed our candle, and, lit with a steady small flame, the vessels floated off downstream with our wishes.

A few years ago, Melany had a heartbreaking experience that changed her life. Her response was a truly inspirational lesson to me: She continued her practice of meditation, mindful breath, and prayers and then resolved—in her fifties—to learn an entirely new skill, the ukulele. "I decided to 'replace the peg,' a Buddhist expression of exchanging fear and stuck feelings with conscious positive thoughts in the present moment," Melany told me. "The past was traumatic and the future was unknown, so the present was the only place I could live." She taught herself the instrument by attending a few workshops, and the process brought needed song and joy back into her life the way she knew it would. "It was a continuation of my habit of being a lifelong learner," she says. Soon after, she started an annual ukulele camp, Tunes in the Dunes—and ninety people showed up the first year. She even got invited to Molokai, Hawaii, to organize other annual retreats there. For me, she's an inspirational example of intentionally shape-

shifting loss to joy, finding and discovering a calling, and creating a livelihood.

And those callings are many and creative and artistic. Melany was trained as a tapestry weaver, and her work adorns the walls; but she weaves people, play, family, and passions into all the meals and gatherings she organizes, as well. Duncan, too, is an exceptional and multitalented artist. He designs graphics and clothing, has written lovely poems and even a children's book about the sea, and photographs beautiful places the way Ansel Adams did with Yosemite—conservation through awe. He and I love to run out and capture magnificent moments together through our lenses. Duncan's love for his watershed inspired him to become more intimate with it, so he took an epic thirty-mile, four-day trek from source to sea, following the way of the salmon. He wrote and photographed and worked with fish biologists and native plant specialists to better understand the inner workings and gifts such ecosystems provide us. "I have observed that insight comes from 'equity of time' spent in a place and focused deeply—like the many seasons of weather we have at Westwind, or the workings of the estuary, or life at the wild edge of a continent where land meets sea," Duncan says. "It inspires me to share through photography, poems, and teaching. It's really an expression of love and of my deep relationship with Cascade Head."

Their garden is yet another manifestation of their connection to place. They harvest salad greens, potatoes, and squash with the best flavor, for family and visitors alike. It's all grown, cooked, blessed, and eaten with love—a full circle of grace. "I like playing with the Earth, watching things grow," Melany says. "Today, the sunflowers are going to bloom; tomorrow, herbs. Food from the garden tastes better. It's connecting to life."

And they never want to stop connecting—or acting on their passions. Duncan, with his prophetic business experience and entrepreneurial spirit, has started ten businesses. His latest is Fishpeople, a sustainable seafood company sourced from their coastal Oregon community, that now supplies progressive grocers throughout the Pacific Northwest and Northern California. It all began with questions: How can we support the fishermen who are committed to sustainable fishing practices? What do families, elders, and young people all want? They want wild-caught, convenient, and delicious seafood, of course. I've had the fun of taste-testing and voting on some recipes Duncan and

Melany cooked up together for Fishpeople. More important, I've witnessed what is involved in taking one idea, growing it, and then actually making it a creative entrepreneurial business: It requires vision, tenacity, commitment, and flexibility.

To align what you love—your ethical and spiritual values—with place, food, work, community, creativity, and joy, and then turn it into a sustainable livelihood, is incredibly inspiring to me. Melany and Duncan stay true to what's important to them. I can see it when we hike steep hillsides and balance on sheer cliffs on Cascade Head, photographing thunderous waves that shake the headlands. I can see it when Duncan shows me how to track stars, taking long exposures as the light moves across the heavens. I can see it when Melany teaches me how to cook, blending late-winter greens and herbs from the garden with wild mussels and crabs we have gathered. Duncan and Melany have become indigenous to this wild place, reading the tides, winds, migrating birds, and the swelling of the tree buds in order to navigate the tidal river, gather food, and plan their days.

Money may come and go, but Duncan and Melany are always philanthropists. They steward what they love with creativity and commitment. It's the kind of generosity that inspires others, that generates ideas, that encourages goodness—and really ripples up from the Source. Melany and Duncan's relationship is respectfully independent and very supportive; they give each other both companionship and space, and they steward one another's dreams and gifts. Their spiritual life, of daily Buddhist meditation and mindful living, is one of their great connectors. When they come back to their breath, they come back to their great love of Nature, family, and the underlying creativity that deepens and weaves us all together. They respond to their callings each and every day, and live always by their family motto: "This moment, only once."

"A lot of wisdom—
especially insight
and compassion—
comes when you
focus deeply."

—Duncan Berry

Lynne and Bill Twist

When Lynne Twist's old friend, economist and author John Perkins, invited her to join him and a group on a trip to Guatemala in the 1990s, she had no idea quite how her life was going to change. They did a drumming circle there with a medicine man to get a glimpse of their calling and their highest life purpose, and she had a vision: being an eagle flying over a rain forest with a small, brown, twisting river. She saw great warrior heads with painted faces and long, black hair with red- and yellow-feathered headbands. Lynne was shocked—she had never had a revelation like this or seen beings like this before.

Decades earlier, John had been with the Peace Corps in Ecuador and worked with the Shuar people. The figures in her vision, he told her, were Achuar warriors, a neigh-

boring tribe to the Shuar. John told Lynne "that the Achuar people are now ready for contact." He said, "We must go to them."

"I'm working in India and Africa," she replied. "I have a lot on my plate. I'm trying to end world hunger, and I don't have time for this. I can't go." It was true: Lynne had been working with the Hunger Project since 1977. She was responsible for fund-raising operations in forty-seven countries. She was, to say the least, busy.

And so she went to a series of meetings in West Africa. As she was convening with her colleagues in Ghana, the painted faces of the Achuar warriors would come to her. It didn't matter whether she was

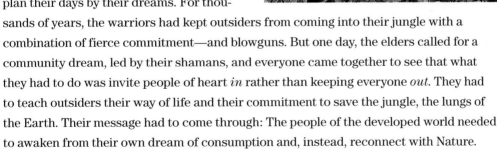

asleep or awake, or where she was in the world. She kept seeing their faces.

In the meantime, John went back to South America with his friend Daniel Koupermann, an ecotourism pioneer, to see the Achuar—and confirmed that these remote indigenous people, threatened by oil development, were ready for contact with the modern world. Soon after, Lynne decided she must go, and she and John brought a group of ten people to visit the Achuar. Lynne's husband, Bill, a business executive, joined them at the last minute.

The Achuar are a dream culture: They plan their days by their dreams. For thousands of years, the warriors had kept outsiders from coming into their jungle with a combination of fierce commitment—and blowguns. But one day, the elders called for a community dream, led by their shamans, and everyone came together to see that what they had to do was invite people of heart *in* rather than keeping everyone *out*. They had to teach outsiders their way of life and their commitment to save the jungle, the lungs of the Earth. Their message had to come through: The people of the developed world needed to awaken from their own dream of consumption and, instead, reconnect with Nature.

It was from the call of the rain forest itself that Lynne and Bill traveled to the

Redreaming the World

Achuar. The trip changed their lives and the lives of thousands of others forever: In 1996, they founded the Pachamama Alliance, dedicated to empowering indigenous peoples of the Amazon rain forest to save both their land and their culture—and teach the rest of the world how to live sustainably and compassionately. They had a joyous life change. It wasn't planned, but it was led by the heart.

It wasn't the first time Lynne had responded to a calling. She first started fund-raising in 1978 for a primary school in the Western Addition of San Francisco, where she moved with Bill after he completed his MBA. ("My husband is just a total and complete hero for me, an incredible, big-hearted, warrior-spirit man," she says.) Just a few years later, she dove into work with the Hunger Project, where she came into contact with Mother Theresa, Desmond Tutu, Maya Angelou, Jane Goodall, and the Dalai Lama. She interacted with people who were living on the very edge of survival in Ethiopia and trying to recover after the 1984–1985 famine.

Since 1996, she has been working with people in the rain forest who were prospering but didn't even know money existed. It is a wonderful challenge. "I really, really know it when I'm in the zone, when I'm a match for the mountain and the mountain is a match for me," she says. And her work gives her "complete joy. It's nourishing. It fills me. It gives me a surge of heart and beauty and nourishment, like a kind of superfood."

All of her experiences led her to global activism and speaking engagements and, finally, to writing *The Soul of Money* in 2003—about how our attitudes toward money can give us insight into the very idea of fortune and success, and how our personal assets are not just lines on a bank statement. "Make a difference with what you have, not seek something you don't have—that is such a nourishing way to live," she says. "What you appreciate will, in fact, appreciate out of the nourishment of your appreciation. The work I do, and the people with whom I do it, regenerate me, and I regenerate them," says Lynne.

Since childhood, I dreamed of exploring the Amazon rain forest. I heard stories from my mom's good friend, who had volunteered there as a nurse in her youth; she spoke of it as we kayaked together in San Francisco Bay. At the turning of the new millennium, I heard Lynne and Bill speak about the Pachamama Alliance, and immediately decided to go with them. A few weeks later, I was flying to Ecuador with our mutual dear friend, Anna Rheim, winding our way through the "valley of seven volcanoes" in the Andes, then into the jungle by a tiny plane, landing on a narrow dirt runway cut by machete. We began our spiritual journey here in the rain forest, one of the most beautiful and diverse places on Earth. I felt at home. I saw rare birds, butterflies, and animals. We met leaders, families, and shamans for a personal introduction into their indigenous way of life and their fierce commitment to their biodiverse home.

Over our twelve-day adventure, I got to know and love the Twists for their impeccable dedication to serve in a loving manner. I so respect how Bill has transformed his business experience, great intellect, heart, and tenacity to serving the global community—and reinventing their own lives. They've inspired countless people to align their daily lifestyles both with their callings and with the dreams of other people around the world. Lynne's energy is boundless, and the Earth is better for it. "I realize being in balance is just not part of my value set," she says. "The juice is in full-throttle living, even when it's tough, even when it's a battle that needs to be waged in order to have something really go the way we all want. It's always, for me, a win-win-win-win situation."

The Twists are just as inspired by, and give energy to, life at home with family. Lynne says that one of the greatest gifts she's ever had in her life is her grandchildren. "To say that I love them is such a small statement for such a big experience that I almost hesitate to say it that way," she says. "When my own three children were little and they made mistakes or their faces were dirty, something was wrong with *me*. I couldn't get my own identity and ego out of the way. But as a grandmother, I can just totally, unconditionally love them." She calls them "love crumbs of the first order."

Her commitment is to help assure a world that's still here for her grandchildren and her great-great-great-grandchildren. And not just something that's left after ravaged generations of unconsciousness—but a renewed place where what we think of as "business" turns into nurturing and serving people, where Nature has rights in court and the true law is natural law, where there's dancing instead of weapons, where there's no money in politics, and "the currency is love and responsibility instead of big money." She imagines a renaissance, like the one that happened in Europe, but this time it will be an absolute reverence for the natural world and a revelation about where human beings see their place in the community of life. Lakes and rivers and skies will return to their natural state. "The bees, the flowers, the trees, the mice, the ants, the wolves, the antelope—they are our sisters and brothers, and we live among them," she says. And humans, themselves, will be equal to each other. "Women will have a coequal partnership with men so that both wings of humanity fly and humanity soars, rather than one wing being weak and the other one overdeveloped and making us fly in circles," she says.

One of the most life-changing aspects of my first trip to Ecuador was that all five of the shamans we met told me I was a medicine woman, and it made me realize I had to step into a new responsibility to support the healing of the Earth with my own gifts and talents. Lynne trained me as a leader, and I have since been there six times. I've taught Achuar youth to paint and illustrate their first book in their own native language, which we published and sent to them. Thanks to the Twists and the Achuar, I was open to a new calling of my own, where spirit and all of life are held in the natural world, where we are all connected, and there's reverence for all people, across the whole spectrum. "You know," Lynne says, "I always think when I'm walking up a hill that gravity is the Earth's love for her creatures, to keep them close. It feels so much better. I'm not trying to fight her. I'm just staying with her as I go up."

**"I've discovered all around me are people
I love more than I can say.
I see partners. I see nothing but 'us.'
There's no 'them' anymore. There's only 'us.'
There's only the beloved, blessed community."**

—Lynne Twist

Lily Yeh

In 1986, the Afro-American dancer/choreographer and educator Arthur Hall made an offer to Lily Yeh that she couldn't refuse: He asked her to develop an empty lot next to his studio in the 2500 block of Germantown Avenue, in the Badlands of North Philadelphia, into a park. He wanted to bring African culture, music, and dance into his neighborhood and into the general public consciousness in order to build pride in African American people and enrich the cultural life of America. Despite apprehension, Lily responded. With a modest $2,500 grant, the Chinese-born artist bought a few garden tools, drew a circle in the middle of the chaos, and began to look for help. Everyone told her she was crazy. Everyone told her it was dangerous. But children came around in droves, asking her, "Hey, lady! Can I help? Let me help!" Jointly, they started to clean and rake the circle, widening it to hold both the darkness and the

light. No matter whether they were drug dealers, addicts, or squatters; whether they stood around a burning fifteen-gallon oil drum to stay warm at night; whether they were homeless; whether—like JoJo, with his chains and knives, who soon became her guide—they might be considered threatening. She invited them all to be part of the project. She didn't judge. Instead, she was delighted that they would come to help her park-building effort, and they together embarked on a new, great experiment.

But it was a long journey to that moment. Lily was originally trained as a traditional Chinese scroll painter, with the Taoist or Buddhist idea of the dustless landscape, tranquil but dynamic, a place of pristine beauty devoid of egohood and human greed. In these works, the natural landscape is sacred and the human figure is typically very tiny and often elderly, walking on a narrow trail next to huge mountains and rivers. They're symbolic of wisdom, of our spiritual path in life, and of our connection to Nature; the scrolls are so peaceful you can meditate on them. In 1963, at just twenty-two years old, Lily was offered a scholarship to attend the Graduate School of Fine Arts at the University of Pennsylvania. She ended up teaching at Philadelphia's University of the Arts for three decades. Her large watercolor flower paintings sold well in galleries, yet she longed for a place to create beauty that would be *lived* in.

    This vision ultimately led Lily to the Badlands. By the third summer, it became clear that the park was her calling and needed her full-time. She eventually quit her teaching job—leaving behind the security of a steady paycheck, health insurance, retirement, and tenure—and traded it for hundred-hour weeks, raising her young son, writing grants, and putting her full spirit into cultivating and growing the Village of Arts and Humanities. Yes, it had blossomed into a village: Together, they created parks, gardens,

Creating Rainbows in Dark Places

and a sense of community. She recruited diverse people to teach music, dance, and the-ater. Teenagers told raw, authentic stories—about drive-by shootings and overdoses—that were turned into plays and performed on the outdoor stage at Ile Ife Park. Neighbors of all ages came out to listen, sitting on blankets and beach chairs. The torn fabric of the community was being rewoven.

Lily's art is far more than just making beautiful murals on the sides of buildings. It includes healing individuals, creating ritual, and enlivening the sacred space with living theater, ceremonies, celebrations, and festivals. On one wall in the Village of the Arts and Humanities, Lily painted Ethiopian angels with swords for protection and taught Big Man, a six-foot-eight drug dealer and addict, to mosaic them into what became Angel Alley, the pride of the whole village. Big Man found his calling, got off drugs, and became an inspiring community artist and youth leader. Sometimes for just a dollar, she

bought burnt-out, slumping buildings—once beautiful, but abandoned after years of economic discrimination and neglect—in the broken neigh-borhood. Counseled by Big Man, Lily employed neighborhood adults to refurbish them for hous-ing, a teen center, and art studios.

What most people would consider a throw-away, whether it's a vacant lot or a human being, Lily sees as an abundance of potential and spirit. "Broken places, broken people, broken promises—there is room for new possibility to create that dustless place," she says. "Mending and repairing brokenness is an inward journey to know the dark and light in myself." A petite woman over seventy years old, she has a childlike curiosity and enchantment; her joyousness is sparked with imagination that blossoms into a beauty that heals and transforms the shattered.

In 1994, she was invited to Korogocho, a settlement outside of Nairobi, Kenya, where some one hundred thousand people scratch out a living sorting through piles of garbage at the dump to find something to recycle. I heard Lily say that if she did not go, she felt as if the most important part of her would die. Lily connects to her heart and musters up passionate courage like no one else I know. She goes forward, knowing that her art is her service, knowing that it can transform a place and a people. That's how she uses her fear: to change it into depth, creativity, and power; to push herself forward. She's remarkable. Her work in Africa inspired her to found Barefoot

Artists in 2002, and since then, it has enriched poor communities around the globe.

Her 2006 project at the Dandelion School outside of Beijing, China, was to transform a very sterile factory-like environment—and to engage 670 students and teachers in the process. With no plants or apparent loveliness, it was the kind of place that would make *me* discouraged and depressed. Yet for Lily, it was opportunity! She began with the children, who had never done art before, and asked them to depict a place of beauty. At first, they produced only muddy, dark paintings. And then she showed them gorgeous cutout folk art from a legendary local Chinese artist, Ku Shu Lan, who had just passed away. "Folk art from all over the world, children's art, and art of ancient times and faraway places inspire my work," she says. "Chinese gardens, African vernacular structures, and Islamic architecture hold a spell over me." Ku Shu Lan's whimsical, bright depictions of cats and flowers delighted the children, too. Lily taught them to paint big and paint together, translating what they saw into colorful pictures on the drab walls, and then how to mosaic the paintings with wheelbarrows full of broken tiles they found in empty lots. "Before we

painted," Lily said, "one child said, 'We tried to imagine what a rainbow would look like on the building. Now the rainbow showers rays of colors. It fills our campus with love.'"

I don't think Lily would say that she is a healer. But in her humble, modest way, with her bag of colorful paints and her magical skills, she ignites beauty that transforms and transcends. She tells stories, sparking new visions and engaging the community into their own imagination. For example, in

the survivor village she transformed in Rwanda, having a milking cow is a dream luxury. When a child drew a cow on a little piece of paper, Lily redrew it to cover the side of a house, and they painted it together—thus visualizing abundance and possibility. Here, in 1994, between eight hundred thousand and a million people were killed over one hundred days of unthinkable violence. She invited survivors to come alive again and honor their loved ones by building a beautiful memorial

genocide park with a bone chamber. It put to rest, with honor and respect, their horrific terrors and living nightmares. Lily brought healing salve to the wound that most believed would never heal. "Making art is a simple act—direct, accessible and effective," she says. "It can take place almost in any place and circumstance. It does not cost a lot and can heal deeply. It creates a new space where people can express themselves and have their voices heard, and where people can dream of possibilities and envision their future."

The Twa people, Rwanda's indigenous potters, live in extreme poverty and have historically been the most persecuted and marginalized. Lily helped them envision and build an art center with a communal kiln to fire their pots. Working with solar engineer Dr. Richard Komp, the villagers learned to make solar panels for electricity. Lily sponsored the installation of water catchments for bathing and drinking. With her courage and fierce, full-hearted love-nature, Lily shape-shifts fear into a fuel that drives her to create and transform the poorest of poor places in Africa, Palestine, India, Haiti, Taiwan, and China—anywhere in the world she is needed.

In between giving her all on international trips, Lily recharges herself with family and Nature—or both, because the best time for her is being with her family in the

mountains, taking a hike or visiting her niece, who is a Buddhist nun in Northern California. It's where she gets nourished to be just who she is. When she visits me, she says, "Oh, Lizzie. I come to heaven and stay with you." We take long walks by the beach and the redwoods. She loves to visit Utah and meet up with her dear friend Terry Tempest Williams, the great naturalist writer who wrote about Lily's Rwanda work in *Finding Beauty in a Broken World*. Being in deep Nature revitalizes her. When she is home in her little house in Philadelphia—making her art, writing grants, meditating, walking in her neighborhood, having a cup of tea or coffee on the corner where people know her, walking through her park—that is recentering to who she is. The slow time at home recharges her.

The first time I went to the Village of Arts and Humanities, about twenty years ago, it felt foreign to me. I'd never seen such poverty in America: blocks of dilapidated buildings, empty lots with piles of debris, folks sitting on stoops, people throwing trash on the ground. It was a completely different cultural experience for me. But as I began to work with Lily there, my perception changed; my fear was transformed into possibility and a sense of community and love. Once, I helped her teach a workshop, and watched as she told children about different cultural guardian spirits, angels, and ancestors. They traced each others' bodies on cloth and then painted themselves as guardian angels—big, beautiful, and powerful. Some had multiple arms or huge wings or fast running shoes. Some of the paintings were turned into colorful banners and hung in the village. One child said his angel was his mom who had died, but he knew she was watching out for him. They all began to realize there is a powerful unseen force they could key in to, to be the biggest and best parts of themselves.

Right now, Lily is working in a Palestinian refugee camp in the West Bank. She invited me to join her there, but the first thing I felt was fear. Once, she had to stop painting because of threats of violence, and I asked her if she was frightened. She said, "No, I am an artist with a paintbrush. I am no threat. That is all I carry." I thought of all the people who carry guns for protection, and here she is, wielding a paintbrush like a magic wand to awaken and bloom a place back with love. Lily has a fighting inner spirit for goodness. She believes everyone has a right to beauty and art. Her childlike glee and enthusiasm is so contagious that it ignites everyone, weaving spirit into each and every moment. Yet everything is done with gestures as simple as bringing crepe paper for children to make headbands and little flags. In the end, the transformations are about celebrations with community, about food, about singing and dancing and fully expressing joy. It is not her creation that is celebrated, but *everybody's* creation, because they have all made sacred space together.

Years ago, I attended a ceremony at night. The youth, all dressed in white gowns with colorful kente cloth sashes, held fiery torches that lit their proud dark faces and made the mosaics sparkle on the walls and terraces. They led the procession, singing gospel through the village to Meditation Park. Twenty teens stood on a platform in a circle facing the community. They took an oath for goodness, and the crowd pledged back to stand behind them. It was truly clear at that moment what I was witnessing: Lily had blossomed into a social artist and a ceremonial artist, someone more magnificent than an alchemist—who, after all, merely changes lead into gold. She, a warrior priestess for the good and true, had turned the broken into a whole of numinous beauty.

And she continues to see abundance in emptiness, because in great poverty, there is great potential. Each tiny piece of tile, thrown away by people, is placed thoughtfully together so that brokenness is made whole through a creative process. Every shard of pottery, discarded metal, and old wood is salvaged and transformed and made valuable again. Like the flower she was named after, Lily has chosen to follow the light.

LIFE MAPPING

for Your Authentic Journey

After following the four pathways, you are an experienced traveler. Using tools and skills from your practices and your experiences, and talents, you'll set the *direction* for the full expression of your true self. You will begin to answer life's most *compelling* questions: Who am I? What do I want? What is my purpose? Using the Life Mapping process, you'll assess your passions and your talents, and give thought to what the world needs. Then you chart these elements to *create* the map to your chosen destination. Every year, friends and I create a Life Map, and we help steward each other's *dreams* and actions to bring clarity to possibilities and directions to dreams. Your intentions will inspire you to *action,* and you'll imbue your life with clarity, purpose, and results.

Your Path to Joy

Is there something you dreamed of doing as a child? Are your life and work fulfilling and meaningful? Are you looking at a career change, just starting or reentering the workforce, or beginning an "encore" in the second half of your life? Are you ready to share your talents and passions with others? Do you feel engaged and appreciated at work and in your community? Is it time to reimagine your life? Have you ever wondered how you can combine what you love with contributing to the world in a meaningful way

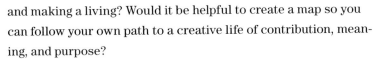

and making a living? Would it be helpful to create a map so you can follow your own path to a creative life of contribution, meaning, and purpose?

Life Mapping is a process that will help you find your personal North Star, guiding you to live an authentic life with passion, meaning, and direction. You'll reflect on how you can stay the course, right yourself, or plan a new route. First, you'll list your passions and all that you love; then you'll identify your unique gifts, talents, and skills. You'll analyze issues that need attention around the world and around your community. You'll set goals with clarity, specificity, and depth; discover where your contributions can impact people, communities, and causes in need of assistance; and uncover where you will find joy and fulfillment.

You'll create your own action plan for weaving together the significant areas of your life: sustaining personal health, spiritual, emotional, and financial satisfaction. As you explore your personal gifts and what you love, you'll create an individual map to guide you in the direction of your dreams and meaningful goals. You will establish daily practices selected from the Four Pathways to support you on your journey and find ways to create actions to braid your passions and your skills with what you feel the world needs.

LIFE ✳ MAPPING

♡ PASSIONS ♡

children · animals
Spiritual depth · Ritual
Creative expression
Photography · Painting
Beauty   Writing
Nature · Friends & family
Travel - Adventure
teaching · Stories
Gardens, gardening
Food
Play
FUN!

♡ SKILLS + TALENTS ♡

Creating Beauty
gardens, Flowers
Celebrations, rituals
Lecturing / teaching
writing, Photography
Painting
Teaching · inspiring others

Creative ideas
Problem solving
Plant knowledge
Monet's Garden expert
Cross-cultural studies

ACTIONS
Write Book LLFB
ACTIONS with photos
Teach + lecture
Green heart Guild
Ritual + story-telling

Spiritual
meditation · community
silence · gratitude prayer

more
Love + Passion
to my personal Life
workshops,
teaching, school
creativity, Sacred
+ Nature to
others
Travel + teach
ART shows to teach
Book To Teach, inspire
Right Livelihood
ACTIONS

PHYSICAL
dance
yoga
swim
hike
health
diet
good
food

ACTIONS
Time in Nature
PLAY
create
reflect
Joy
Complete Book + Photos.
design website +
workshops + online teaching
Community Rituals
Nature + Sacred
ART · creativity express
Love of Nature

MENTAL

EMOTIONAL

— ACTIONS —

♥ LOVE ♥
Connection of the Sacred to ALL Life
People · Places · Nature
Deep health of Earth & People
Connection to & Respect of Nature
STOP Climate change
FALL IN Love with EARTH!

♡ What The World Needs ♡

North STAR
☆ Depth & Clarity

LIFE MAPPING FOR YOUR AUTHENTIC JOURNEY **187**

Getting Started on Your Life Map

You may want to sit in silence for a few minutes to center yourself. Perhaps you'll want to light a candle or sip some tea. Allow your mind to be at rest. Give yourself the gift of time to explore your future. Making a Life Map can take a few hours, a few days, or more.

MATERIALS

**Notebook
(or the artist sketchbook from your practices)**

**Large sheet of paper, such as
25 x 30-inch easel paper**

Large, round dinner or serving plate to trace

Colored pens or pencils

Exploring Your Story

In developing a map as a guide for your life path to the future, you'll need to assess where you're at today. To fully capture the scope of your life—your interests, gifts, and thoughts—think about and write answers to the following questions: What are your passions? What are your skills and talents? What do you think the world needs? Reflect on the Four Pathways and the practices that really touched or inspired you; these may be areas to bring into your Life Map. After reading the stories of the Full Bloomers, you may be inspired to try a new skill, like playing the ukulele, or start a green business or volunteer for a community project locally or internationally. Write your insights, ideas, and answers on different pages in the notebook. Make your responses as personal as possible. Perhaps you'll need more than one session to record all your thoughts and build your lists. I've included sample seed words to help you get started and see the possible scope of the exercise. Feel free to borrow these words—many of them came from my Life Mapping workshops!

WHAT ARE YOUR PASSIONS?

What do you love? Perhaps you have a deep love of the Earth or heartfelt compassion for children or animals or love the thrill of adventure and travel. Maybe you have a creative streak or an affinity for music, sports, different cultures, baking, or knitting. Passions are often those things that are at the leading edge of your life—not necessarily what you are good at yet, but those things that get you excited and make you feel awake and alive. Is it folk music, rock 'n' roll, classical music—or none of the above? Do you love to garden, read, write poetry, or engage in local politics? What about tennis, dance, running, or meditation? If you could sign up for a class at a university or community college (and your grade wouldn't matter), what would you want to learn? How about juggling, archery, geocaching, photography, painting, social networking, a foreign language, winemaking, or anthropology? In your notebook, make a list of whatever feels exciting and curious!

Seed Words for Passions

Consider what you love—hobbies, volunteering, reading, conversations, travel—and you'll identify your passions. Sometimes what you love may have been on the back burner as your life had other priorities, but passions are things you've always yearned to do and explore. Be passionate!

family	sailing	exploring	biking
ecology	horseback riding	rituals	woodworking
travel	celebrations	flower arranging	camping
music	clean energy	church groups	organic gardening
play and fun	wildlife conservation	birding	open space
art	social justice	skiing	activism
antiquing	being a locavore	computers	stamp collecting
beauty	volunteering	hosteling	board games
elders	knitting	animals	thrift shopping
learning new things	community involvement	politics	foraging
oceans		mentoring	historic preservation

WHAT ARE YOUR SKILLS AND TALENTS?

List all your gifts and talents, such as making soup, gardening, leading meetings, and being a good listener. Don't be shy about the attributes that you share at home, at work, or in your community. This is the "tool kit" (or assets) you've developed over the years, and it is unique to you!

Many women are very modest and discount their abilities. They can be stumped at this exercise, saying, "Oh, that doesn't count. Anyone could do that!" Some people have a worthiness issue, but it is important to really stand behind your own magnificence. A retired woman had been an office manager for thirty years and didn't mention it. Many people overlook skills they used in raising a family or being a volunteer or they learned early in life. Perhaps you have a long list of talents to share. It can be helpful to engage another person in conversation about your life, so ask a friend to help you create your list. It is a wonderful gift to be recognized and reminded of the skills and talents you offer.

Seed Words for Skills and Talents

Think about all the jobs you've held in your life, all of the people you've helped, and all of the things you do at home. Think about times you've volunteered, collaborated, and initiated a change. Know thyself.

writing	cooking	letter writing	working with children and youth
playing music	healing	teaching	sales
cross-cultural knowledge	inspiring others	sports	building and repairing
research	typing	coaching and encouraging others	idea generation
humor	organizing	problem solving	acting
positive thinking	listening	creativity	investing
farming/ranching	counseling	party planning	computer skills
public speaking	storytelling	caretaking	martial arts
kayaking	foreign languages	communication	food preservation
visualizing	photography	networking	
	spelling		

WHAT DO YOU THINK THE WORLD NEEDS?

You'll probably want to list the big things like peace, equality, and abundant food, but be sure to add personal insights that reflect your values and interests. Be very pragmatic and specific and think both globally and locally. Maybe your vision includes an heirloom seed bank, climate stabilization, and a connection to spirit in Nature. What do you think could be improved in the world? Did you recognize a need while traveling or have you held a concern in your heart for years but didn't think you'd be able to do anything about it?

Think about your own region and neighborhood. What are the needs you see every day, and, more specifically, who is in need? You probably see opportunities nearby (schools, elderly, litter, or recycling) but haven't considered how to act on them. Does your community need help resettling immigrants, tree planting, revitalizing abandoned properties, re-envisioning a city's future? Think big, think small, think infrastructure, think people. Be specific; list things you can grab on to and make your own.

Seed Words for What the World Needs

Scan the world and local news, read a newspaper, or talk with someone in a position of power in the community, and you'll quickly identify issues in need of attention and possible solutions. Be the visionary!

love	renewable energy sources	inspiration	good health for all people
peace	appreciation for what we have	globally sustainable practices	art for everyone
equality	integrity with leadership	indigenous wisdom combined with modern knowledge	ecological education
social justice	girls' rights	humane treatment of animals	community resilience
access to education	hope	recognition of the Creator in all of Creation	food for all
climate stabilization	commitment to the good, true, and beautiful	joy and happiness	rights for Nature
respect for diversity	stable governments	worldwide cooperation	sustainable transportation
spiritual fulfillment	conservation of Earth's resources		female leaders
adequate shelter			earth justice
clean water			public libraries
opportunity			
religious tolerance			

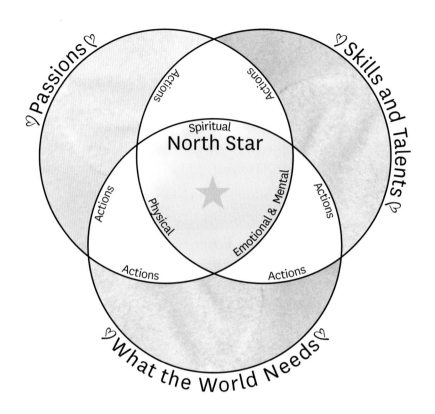

Creating Your Life Map

With your lists recorded in your notebook, it's time to bring all of your ideas together to create a Life Map. On your paper, trace the plate three times, overlapping two circles on the top and one on the bottom. The overlaps will create one center triangle and three side triangles. Use the Life Map pattern as a guide.

Add labels to the Life Map—the top left circle is *Passions*, the top right circle is *Skills and Talents*, and the bottom circle is *What the World Needs*. Color *Passions* pink, *Skills and Talents* blue, and *What the World Needs* green. Label the middle triangle *North Star* and draw a yellow star in it. Label the three side triangles *Actions*.

FILLING IN THE CIRCLES

Study your lists and notice if you have any connections between your *Passions*, *Skills and Talents*, and *What the World Needs* circles or if they are all seemingly unconnected. Circle or color the connections or themes you track; this usually indicates your life is more integrated and aligned. Don't judge—just notice.

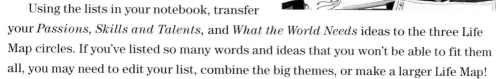

Using the lists in your notebook, transfer your *Passions*, *Skills and Talents*, and *What the World Needs* ideas to the three Life Map circles. If you've listed so many words and ideas that you won't be able to fit them all, you may need to edit your list, combine the big themes, or make a larger Life Map!

My first maps were crowded with all that I love and do. After making and following my maps for a number of years, I found that it was clearer for me to simplify and just write the biggest themes on my map. I let go of and combined some things. I've noticed that some people in my workshops like to leave a lot of white space and only put down a few key words. There are others with tons of words that completely cover their maps. We can all gaze into a clear mirror to see our true selves and come to a place of loving acceptance and discernment to own what is true for us.

FINDING CONNECTIONS

Your next step is to find connections between the three circles. You may want to highlight any themes you see connecting two or three circles. You may have a life that's braided with the things you love and the gifts and talents you possess. For example, you may have a great love of children and creative expression and your gifts and skills have inspired you to become an elementary school art teacher. Or you may have kept your passions, like golf or hiking, and your skills, like business management or practicing law, separate.

Themes or connections may be obvious, or perhaps they'll be difficult to pinpoint, especially if your personal life and work life are quite separate. It is powerful to put your Life Map on a wall or bulletin board and glance at it over time. Invite a friend to take a look, because she/he may see similar themes in the circles that you haven't identified. Keep these connections in mind as you move to the action steps. I'm now able to view someone's map and see clear connections and possible pathways between the different areas of their Life Map; it's so exciting to help someone discover meaningful direction.

PLANNING FOR ACTION

Now it's time to consider how to transform your passions, skills, and hopes for the world, your community, and yourself into action plans. It may be helpful to work with a partner on this step so you can discuss ideas and inspire one another when identifying and deciding on actions. This is an exciting creative process, and you may find that you don't have instant answers. Take a break, walk outside, have some tea, and be reflective in order for your intuition to be accessed and your guidance to become clear.

When you overlapped your *Passions* and *Skills and Talents* circles, you created a side triangle that allows you to identify actions that would pair your passions with the skills and talents you possess. Think about the connections between the two circles, then consider ways you can integrate your passions with your particular expertise to create action steps for your life.

The side triangle between *Skills and Talents* and *What the World Needs* will show you how to combine the things you do well with a service, business, or offering needed in the world or your community. You've identified common connections in the two circles, so dream of ways you can create positive change and contribution.

The third triangle between *Passions* and *What the World Needs* will allow you to match what you love with global or local concerns to address situations and issues that affect people and places with your inspired vision.

You may have just one action in each triangle or you may have filled your triangles with viable actions you can consider. Some actions may be crystal clear and others may need more thought or time to "tool up" and gain skills in that area. You may be confident about some actions and hesitant about others. Ponder what you've written, share it with others, and let the ideas develop. Your actions will become clear, distinctive, and doable.

You may want to make a list of actions, in order of priority, and break down the action into micro steps to help you accomplish your goal. Consider a timeline, and always plan ways to celebrate big and small completions and accomplishments along the way.

FINDING YOUR NORTH STAR

The center triangle is your North Star—your heart compass. It is like the balancing point of a compass, the place that is true and steady no matter what. Like your truth, values, and morals, it's what you can return to. It can steer you when you are in new territory or need assurance to discern your way. For some, it may be a quality like truth, integrity, or practicing gratitude, or a centering action like conscious breath in silence, sipping a cup of tea mindfully, or prayer. It may also be a quality you are working on.

I have worked for two years with clarity and depth to keep me focused and to realize my many passions and concerns. When I get pulled in many directions and want to "do it all," I remind myself to focus and be clear. Will this opportunity pull me toward align-

ment, enrich my life, and make a difference in the world? Some of us feel like we have attention deficit disorder with all of our distractions, or we get forgetful, too busy, or too lazy and slip into a situation where we are "getting by" rather than clearly choosing to focus on what we love and what we want to contribute to.

Ask yourself: What is at the core of your being? What supports you in combining all these ideas to create your best self? Whatever the quality or intention, write the words or draw the symbol in the North Star triangle. This will keep you focused on achieving your goals and becoming the person whom you wish to be, doing what you love, using untapped potential, and making a contribution.

Look for inspiration in the practices of the Four Pathways. What did you find meaningful in Gardener, Artist, Lover, and Spirit-Weaver? Browse back through your journal

and the ideas in the daily practices and see which ones really resonated for you and which ones you have incorporated into your life. Perhaps it was being in gratitude, keeping a meditation practice, spending time in Nature, making a collage, or dancing. Identify qualities that get you back to your true self when you are stressed, too busy, depressed, or overwhelmed.

In my workshops, I've found that many people find it difficult to define their North Star. It's important to reflect on the qualities that will help you balance health, spirituality, emotions, and finances. Some people are deeply spiritual and healthy but lack financial stability, which causes them stress. Others may have spent a good deal of their time and energy on their livelihood and perhaps neglected their health, families, or spiritual life. Life Mapping is an exercise in self-reflection, allowing you to notice where you can make adjustments. It's just like walking in a foreign place; you need to look at a map throughout the journey, take a few turns, meander back, and find your way to your destination. I was recently traveling by car in France and we loaded a museum address into the GPS. There were long stretches when we were on the right road and didn't need directions, but we were guided by the GPS when we drove through an unfamiliar city with all of its distractions, road closures, and obstacles to find our intended museum.

Think of your North Star as your personal GPS. Punch in where you want to go and the route you want to take, and know that you can get back on course if you take a wrong turn. And you just might find an unexpected miracle along the way.

From Passion to Action

You may find it helpful to see how you could take something you love and a skill that you have to make a contribution to the world, transforming intention to action.

PASSIONS	SKILLS AND TALENTS	WHAT THE WORLD NEEDS
bird watching		knowledge
Nature	bird identification	love
children	gardening	commitment to Nature
teaching	Nature travel	children spending time in Nature
hiking	public speaking	halt to global warming
gardens	patience	world peace
travel	teaching	

EXAMPLE OF POSSIBLE ACTIONS

I can connect my life and my love of birds with community service.

I am going to explore starting a bird watching club with my local library or youth center. The club will be for everyone, but I will target families and youth to deepen their love and knowledge of nature.

I will set up bird feeders and binoculars by a window. We will take walks to observe, listen to, and begin to identify the bird species we see and hear. I will discuss habitat, food sources, behavior, flight patterns, and birdsong identification. I will emphasize the interconnections of birds, plants, and habitats.

We can plant native plants for food and shelter around the library (or center) and our homes.

We can have a feather and nest collection on display.

I will find out what is required to officially teach science or get an Audubon certification to teach.

I may have to "tool up" to have greater impact and make a more meaningful contribution, like taking a beginner's birding class to see how they introduce the concept of birding in fun, easy steps.

I will collect binoculars so families can borrow them, and I will learn smartphone apps to bridge the tech world and the natural world for savvy kids.

I should check into logistics about insurance and clearances to interact with the public.

I know there are many steps to take an idea to the next level of completion. I will create a list of micro action steps and a realistic timeline so I don't get discouraged or overwhelmed.

I will keep checking back with my Life Map and keep my goals in mind as I follow my North Star.

I will celebrate my accomplishments along the way.

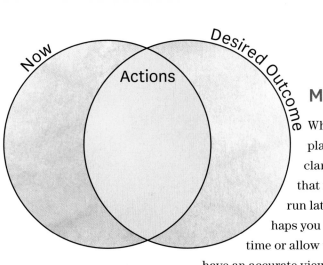

Now

Desired Outcome

Actions

Making a Balance Map

While Life Mapping helps you create an *overall* plan for moving forward, a Balance Map will help clarify *specific* situations and support you in areas that may be troubling. For example, do you tend to run late and try to jam too many things into a day? Perhaps you want to make a change and arrive at work on time or allow time for yourself each day. Or maybe you don't have an accurate view of where your money goes. Perhaps it's time to make a budget and start to save. Do you have extra weight or stress or obligations that could use an overhaul? Creating a Balance Map lets you recognize and shift areas that are "stuck"—it's like taking the kink out of the garden hose so the water can flow with ease. You'll assess where you're at *Now*, identify your *Desired Outcome*, and plan your *Action*. Draw a balance map and label the areas as shown here.

HONEST ASSESSMENT: **WHERE ARE YOU NOW?**

Make a Balance Map for each situation you wish to change, realign, or take action on. Choose one area to work on first (perhaps it's finances, spirituality, health, family, work, time, or leisure activities). In the *Now* circle, write a clear and honest assessment of the situation. If you want to tackle time and lateness issues, perhaps you'll write, "I always run late" or "I always overdo" or "I'm tired of rushing around."

BIG DREAMS: **WHAT IS YOUR DESIRED OUTCOME?**

What do you consider the ideal result or a situation you can live with? If you're tired of being late, you can write as your goal "Being on time, even 5 minutes early" or "Doing less so I leave with enough time to arrive punctually." You may realize that there is more than one desired outcome for a situation.

How can you move from your current situation and condition to your desired outcome? For time and lateness issues, you may have to give up the idea that you can do everything, streamline your morning routine, be more realistic about how long something takes, leave earlier, or just say no when asked for your time. List your actions, and be as specific and as clear as possible. Think about simple, small steps. You are moving out of "stuckness" to empowerment, creating actions for positive change.

OPEN YOURSELF TO TRANSFORMATION

Each one of us has a different story and a unique way of approaching change. Using a Balance Map can help you analyze your situation and guide you to results, regardless of whether you embrace or avoid change. If you feel tired and emotionally drained, you might dream of feeling healthy, keeping your body flexible, riding your bike, and doing yoga. If you've overextended yourself financially, perhaps you want to pay off credit cards and have a savings account for vacations and emergencies. If your family relationships are a little bumpy, maybe you desire meaningful conversations and a healthier way to interact. Create a Balance Map to help you get there.

Balance Maps can be used for your individual situations, but it's equally effective for couples, families, and organizations. Invite others to contribute to the *Now* assessments, the *Desired Outcome*, and the *Actions*. Make a separate Balance Map for each area in your life that you want to improve. It's helpful to look at the action steps and to select one step to focus on for the first month. Implementing change is exciting and satisfying, but concentrate on one issue at a time so you don't become overwhelmed or discouraged. Identify where you want to start, and begin a positive shift today!

Acknowledgments

My full-hearted appreciation to my precious friends, family, and teachers for being the patient caretakers of my heart, soul, and spirit.

I have written this book with much guidance, prayer, and gratitude. I have drawn inspiration from my Irish ancestors and their fierce connection to the sacredness of the land, and from my late parents, who nurtured me early in life and showed me compassion and appreciation.

I want to thank my teacher and mentor for two decades, cultural anthropologist Angeles Arrien, PhD, for her exemplary guidance in cross-cultural traditions, love, and service to others. I also want to express thanks to my late mentor Kathleen Burgy, who guided me for more than forty years with her wisdom, ever-expanding heart, and humor.

My deep gratitude to the Full Bloomers who so graciously allowed me to feature them in this book. Thank you for the love, inspiration, and luminescence that has helped to guide my path.

Betty Peck and her family, daughter Anna Rainville and granddaughters Merina and Sarah, for sharing their consistent wisdom and rhythm of life with love

Lita and Dave Judge, for bringing children to nature

Terry and David Reeves, for community weaving with creativity and generosity

Lynne and Bill Twist, for mentoring my first two life-changing trips to the Amazon rain forest and bringing me into the work of Pachamama Alliance

Lily Yeh, for illuminating dark places with beauty and art that transforms

And special appreciation and gratitude to Melany and Duncan Berry for sharing family, ceremonies, retreats, weekly meditations, check-ins, and support with photography, nuturing, and vision. Thank you for introducing the Life Mapping process to me (Duncan and Fran Macy originally designed it as a nexus process during a Joanna Macy

30-day retreat)—what you hold in your hands is the result of following my Life Map.

I am blessed with a wealth of family and friends who are family, and I share my gratitude with:

My brothers and sisters, nieces and nephew, especially Mary and Thomas who always checked in with encouragement

Ellie Rilla and Janey Ady, for their consistent belief in me and their support of my vision, and for living all four pathways and encouraging communities to bloom with joy

Sandy Rader and Elaine Schegel, garden artists who weave family with beauty and celebration

Margot Grych, Kay Cline, Debra Davalos, and Roelof and Virginia Wijbrandus, Spirit Family, for their generosity of ideas, skills, and mutual support with mirth and merit

Jo Anderson and The Bear Sisters, who took my first weekend Full Bloom workshop to try out the practices

Nancy Mellon, storyteller and neighbor who continues to give me cheer and resolve

Jeff and Susan Turner, Ayurvedic practitioners and good friends who keep me healthy

Dr. Ed Jarvis, poet, healer, and bagpiper

David Feese, spiritual seeker and healer

Marty Newman, dream builder

Jeanne Cameron, who is a Full Bloomer in each of the four pathways: flower artist, photographer, lover, and ritual maker

And cousins Derrie Murray, who exemplifies Irish charm and grace, Brenda Halbrook, and Anne Kilkenny; Patrick O'Neil, who models impeccable character and meaningful conversation; Annie Avery, a friend since the rain forest; Jody Snyder and Noel Littlejohn, who live in Full Bloom; Anna Rheim and Jane Olin, who, along with me, are the Tres Amigas; Penny Allport, who breathes her dreams into being; Matt Regan, FC (faux coach); Cristin DeVine, Nia dance teacher of embodied joy; Gina Puccinelli, yoga teacher who weaves community with health; Jay Tully and family—you are a delight; Mark Brown, my passionate gardening friend in France; my beautiful spirit daughters—Becky Murray, Sahara Saude-Bigelow, and Julie Jensen, who have given me the joy of loving them; Linda Sivertsen, "book whisperer" who helped me form my ideas into a viable proposal; and Dewitt Jones, who inspired me with iPhoneography, my favorite creative tool.

A shout-out of deep appreciation and gratitude to Kenny Ausubel and Nina Simons, founders of the Bioneers Conference, which inspires, informs, and unites our collective reimagining and actions to live on the Earth in ways that honor the web of life, each other, and future generations. This is my tribe!

Much gratitude to Ethne Clarke, who embraced my vision for this book and took the idea to Rodale, where she is editor-in-chief of *Organic Gardening* magazine and planted the seeds of this concept with Executive Editor Karen Bolesta and the Rodale family. It's full circle indeed. I left home at eighteen to garden in Maine, always relying on the classic *Rodale's Organic Gardening* book. My full appreciation to Karen for editing and cultivating *Living Life in Full Bloom* with dedication, tenacity, skill, and respect. My immense gratitude to Art Director Carol Angstadt for patiently and creatively shaping this volume into a beautiful breathing form. Roxanne Buck helped me edit the first practices of the Gardener and Artist pathways, and Janis Daddona copyedited with humor and skill in the first rounds. My appreciation to Senior Project Editor Hope Clarke and copy editors Susan Hindman and Beth Bazar for your careful eye.

Thank you to everyone I photographed and wrote about in my practices. You bring joy to my life and spirit, beauty, and authenticity to *Living Life in Full Bloom*. It takes a community to make a book and to inspire a person to fully bloom. Thank you all.

Resources

BOOKS

**Arrien, Angeles, PhD—
www.angelesarrien.com**
*The Four-Fold Way: Walking the Paths of the
Warrior, Teacher, Healer and Visionary*
(HarperSanFrancisco, 1993)
*Living in Gratitude: A Journey That Will
Change Your Life* (Sounds True, Inc., 2011)
*The Nine Muses: A Mythological Path to
Creativity* (Tarcher, 2000)
*The Second Half of Life: Opening the Eight
Gates of Wisdom* (Sounds True, Inc., 2007)

**Berthoin, Paola Fiorelle, Laura Bayless, and
John Dotson, eds.**
*Passion for Place: Community Reflections on
the Carmel River Watershed* (RisingLeaf
Impressions, 2012) www.passion4place.net

Braza, Jerry
*The Seeds of Love: Growing Mindful Relation-
ships* (Tuttle, 2011); with a foreword by Thich
Nhat Hanh

Capacchione, Lucia
*The Power of Your Other Hand: A Course in
Channeling the Inner Wisdom of the Right
Brain* (New Page Books, 2001)

Estés, Clarissa Pinkola, PhD
*The Faithful Gardener: A Wise Tale about That
Which Can Never Die* (HarperSanFrancisco,
1995)
Women Who Run with the Wolves (Ballantine
Books, 1995)

Fox, Matthew—www.matthewfox.org
*Creativity: Where the Divine and the Human
Meet* (Tarcher, 2002)

Goody, Jack
*The Culture of Flowers (*Cambridge University
Press, 1993)

Harman, Jay
*The Shark's Paintbrush: Biomimicry and How
Nature Is Inspiring Innovation* (White Cloud
Press, 2013)

Johnson, Wendy
*Gardening at the Dragon's Gate: At Work in the
Wild and Cultivated World* (Bantam Books,
2008)

Koren, Leonard
*Wabi-Sabi for Artists, Designers, Poets & Phi-
losophers* (Stone Bridge Press, 1994)

Ladinsky, Daniel, translator
*The Gift: Poems by Hafiz the Great Sufi Mas-
ter* (Penguin Compass, 1999)
*Love Poems from God: Twelve Sacred Voices
from the East and West* (Penguin Compass,
2002)

Levoy, Gregg
*Callings: Finding and Following an Authentic
Life* (Harmony, 1997)

Louv, Richard
*Last Child in the Woods: Saving Our Children
from Nature-Deficit Disorder* (Algonquin
Books, 2008)
*The Nature Principle: Reconnecting with Life
in a Virtual Age* (Algonquin Books, 2012)

Macy, Joanna, and Molly Young Brown
*Coming Back to Life: Practices to Reconnect
Our Lives, Our World* (New Society Publish-
ers, 1998); foreword by Matthew Fox

Mellon, Nancy
Storytelling & the Art of Imagination
(Element, 1992)

Nachmanovitch, Stephen
Free Play: Improvisation in Life and Art
(Tarcher, 1990)

Nye, Naomi Shihab
19 Varieties of Gazelle: Poems of the Middle East (Greenwillow Books, 2002)

O'Donohue, John
Anam Cara: A Book of Celtic Wisdom
(HarperCollins, 1997)
Beauty: The Invisible Embrace (Harper Perennial, 2005)
To Bless the Space Between Us: A Book of Blessings (Doubleday, 2008)

Oliver, Mary
New and Selected Poems, Volume One (Beacon Press, 1992)
New and Selected Poems, Volume Two (Beacon Press, 2004)

Osbon, Diane K., editor
Reflections on the Art of Living: A Joseph Campbell Companion (Harper Perennial, 1991)

Perrow, Susan
Healing Stories for Challenging Behaviour
(Hawthorn Press, 2008)

Pink, Daniel H.
A Whole New Mind: Why Right-Brainers Will Rule the Future (Riverhead Books, 2006)

Plotkin, Bill
Nature and the Human Soul: Cultivating Wholeness and Community in a Fragmented World (New World Library, 2007)

Remen, Rachel Naomi
Kitchen Table Wisdom: Stories That Heal
(Riverhead Books, 1997)
My Grandfather's Blessings: Stories of Strength, Refuge, and Belonging (Riverhead Books, 2000)

Richo, David
How to Be an Adult in Relationships: The Five Keys to Mindful Loving (Shambhala, 2002)

Swimme, Brian Thomas, and Mary Evelyn Tucker
Journey of the Universe (Yale University Press, 2011) (part of a larger project that includes a film, educational DVD series, and Web site, www.journeyoftheuniverse.org)

Swimme, Brian, and Thomas Berry
The Universe Story
(HarperSanFrancisco, 1992)

Taylor, Jill Bolte
My Stroke of Insight: A Brain Scientist's Personal Journey (Viking, 2008)

Tolle, Eckhart
A New Earth: Awakening to Your Life's Purpose (Dutton, 2005)

Williams, Terry Tempest
Finding Beauty in a Broken World
(Pantheon Books, 2008)
When Women Were Birds (Picador, 2013)

Ziegler, Mel, Bill Rosenzweig, and Patricia Ziegler
The Republic of Tea: How an Idea Becomes a Business (The Republic of Tea, 1992)

FILMS/VIDEOS

Ashes and Snow
www.ffilms.org/ashes-and-snow-2005/

Gratitude, The Beauty of Pollination,
and a collection of films by Louie Schwartzberg
www.movingart.com

Journey of the Universe
www.storyoftheuniverse.org

Rivers and Tides
www.riversandtides.co.uk

Story of Stuff
www.storyofstuff.org/movies-all/story-of-stuff/

ORGANIZATIONS

American Friends Service Committee
www.afsc.org
This Quaker organization works with people at
home and around the world for peace and
social justice. I began volunteering with them
at age sixteen.

Bioneers
www.bioneers.org
Bioneers hosts an annual three-day conference
on the advancement of holistic education
pertaining to global social, cultural, and environmental issues. It invites us to reimagine
how to live on Earth in ways that honor the
web of life, each other, and future generations. I attend annually—all lectures are
recorded and available. This is a marvelous
resource for inspiring information and
community.
Moonrise Women's Leadership, a subset of
Bioneers, focuses on leadership that is
sourced from each woman's deep love and
passionate commitment—for the natural
world, women, health, children, the sacred,
and justice.

Esalen Institute
www.esalen.org
Esalen is an integral learning environment devoted
to pioneering deep change in self and society.

Institute of Play
www.instituteofplay.org
The Institute of Play's mission is to promote game
design, games, and gaming as a model tool to
enhance personal and social development.

Thomas Berry Foundation
www.thomasberry.org
Berry was a Catholic priest of the Passionist
order, a cultural historian, and an ecotheolo-
gian who said, "The universe is a communion
of subjects, not a collection of objects." All of
Berry's books and recordings clearly see all of
Creation as spiritual from a Christian perspective.

Wake Up Festival
www.wakeupfestival.com
A celebration of inspirational and new ideas,
weaving intimacy with spirit, Nature, and
community.

PEOPLE

Macy, Joanna, PhD
www.joannamacy.net
This ecophilosopher is a scholar of Buddhism,
general systems, and deep ecology, as well as
a respected voice in the movements for peace,
justice, and ecology.

Schwartzberg, Louie
www.movingart.com
This award-winning cinematographer tells stories of Nature's beauty on film with childlike
wonder and precision. See also his video
Gratitude on YouTube and his profile on
www.ted.com.

Thich Nhat Hanh
www.plumvillage.org and www.deerpark
monastery.org

He is one of the best-known and most respected Zen masters in the world today, a poet, and a peace and human rights activist.

TED: IDEAS WORTH SPREADING

Ted Talks
www.ted.com
Riveting talks by remarkable people you can listen to and be inspired by! Poke around and find your own favorites. These are my top ten:

Louie Schwartzberg: *Nature. Beauty. Gratitude.*

Jill Bolte Taylor: *My Stroke of Insight*

Isabel Allende: *Tales of Passion*

Julie Taymor: *Spider-Man, The Lion King,* and *Life on the Creative Edge*

Viktor Frankl: *Why to Believe in Others*

Elizabeth Gilbert: *Your Elusive Creative Genius*

Sir Ken Robinson: *How Schools Kill Creativity* and *Bring on the Learning Revolution*

Brené Brown: *The Power of Vulnerability* and *Listening to Shame*

Chimamanda Ngozi Adichie: *The Danger of a Single Story*

Karen Armstrong: *My Wish: The Charter for Compassion*

WEB SITES

Big Sur Spirit Garden
www.bigsurspiritgarden.com
Jayson Fann, musician and artist, is director of these international multicultural educational programs and performances across the globe. Check out his spirit nest on page xv.

Butterflies and Moths of North America
www.butterfliesandmoths.org
A one-stop database on butterflies and moths that scientists can use to form or to address research questions, as well as assemble high-quality data on the insects' distribution.

Caring Economy Campaign
www.caringeconomy.org
Founded by Dr. Riane Eisler (www.rianeeisler.com), this organization strives to lay the foundation for a more just, sustainable, and caring economy and world.

Children & Nature Network
www.childrenandnature.org
Reconnecting children and Nature.

Earth Peoples United
www.earthpeoplesunited.org
Connecting people to the natural and spiritual world, and bridging the wisdom of the Ancient Ones with the world of today, so that the diversity of life can flourish for the future.

Encore.org
www.encore.org
Helping others find passion, purpose, and a paycheck in the second half of life.

Evolving Wisdom
www.evolvingwisdom.com
Online educational opportunities guide you through a process of transformation.

Extraordinary Conversations
www.extraordinaryconversations.com
In-depth conversations, collaborations, conflict resolution, and vision making created by Patrick O'Neill (one of my mentors) and his team for individuals and organizations.

Gratefulness.org
www.gratefulness.org
An international nonprofit organization providing resources for living in the gentle power of gratefulness, which restores courage, reconciles relationships, and heals the Earth.

Houston, Jean
www.jeanhouston.org
A scholar, philosopher, and researcher who
offers online courses, workshops, lectures,
and books on social artistry, human potential,
and action.

Hubbard, Barbara Marx
www.barbaramarxhubbard.com
Her Foundation for Conscious Evolution offers
visions of a universal humanity.

Institute of Noetic Sciences
www.noetic.org
Started after astronaut Edgar Mitchell returned
from seeing Earth from the moon and had
a deep spiritual experience, bringing scientific study with consciousness, spirituality,
and wisdom to retreats, publications, and
a conference.

Journey of the Universe
www.journeyoftheuniverse.org
Excellent resource for linking cosmology,
mythology, religions of the world, and deep
ecology—for personal growth and teaching.

Lady Bird Johnson Wildflower Center
www.wildflower.org
Working to increase the sustainable use and
conservation of native wildflowers, plants,
and landscapes.

National Garden Bureau
www.ngb.org
Growing information for specific plants.

The Nature Conservancy
www.nature.org
Works to conserve lands and waters and provides a free carbon footprint calculator
(www.nature.org/greenliving/carboncalculator
/index.htm) to measure your impact on the
climate—and gives you ideas for lowering it.

Organic Gardening
www.organicgardening.com
Organic Gardening magazine brings you expert
garden advice and shows how to use natural
and organic garden methods.

Parabola
www.parabola.org
A quarterly magazine where spiritual
traditions meet.

Plant Conservation Alliance
www.nps.gov/plants
Consortium of agencies and individuals working
to solve the problems of native plant extinction and native habitat restoration, ensuring
the preservation of our ecosystem.

Pollan, Michael
www.michaelpollan.com
Author and visionary about food and our
relationship with the Earth—all of his books
are great and important.

Pollinator Partnership
www.pollinator.org
The largest organization in the world dedicated
to the protection and promotion of pollinators
and their ecosystems.

Positive News
www.positivenewsus.org
News that brings hope, exemplifies
solutions, and inspires action.

Rodale Institute
www.rodaleinstitute.org
Dedicated to pioneering organic farming
through research and outreach.

Seeds of Success
www.nps.gov/plants/sos
Working to collect, conserve, and develop native
plant materials for stabilizing, rehabilitating,
and restoring lands in the United States.

Seed Savers Exchange
www.seedsavers.org
Preserving heirloom plant varieties through regeneration, distribution, and seed exchange.

ServiceSpace
www.servicespace.org
A social media network that helps you change yourself, then change the world, with projects and Web sites about service, kindness, and good news.

USDA Natural Resources Conservation Service
www.plants.usda.gov and www.nrcs.usda.gov
Excellent resources for plants in the United States, including 40,000 images and lists for pollinators.

Women's Earth Alliance
www.womensearthalliance.org
Promotes clean water, healthy food, and protected land in impacted communities worldwide through strategic investments in women's leadership at the grassroots level.

***YES!* Magazine**
www.yesmagazine.org
Powerful positive and practical ideas and stories to promote action.

SERVICE PORTALS

Awakin.org (a project of ServiceSpace)
A curated repository of secular wisdom that offers people a chance to explore their own life and experiences more deeply via insightful readings, weekly call-in programs with inspiring guests, and meditation communities.

CFSites.org (a project of ServiceSpace)
A user-friendly tool that enables people involved in good work to create custom Web sites at no charge.

Conversations.org (a project of ServiceSpace)
A collection of in-depth interviews with artists from all walks of life.

DailyGood.org (a project of ServiceSpace)
Uplifting news stories are delivered in a unique package from this site to more than 100,000 inboxes around the world each day for free.

KarmaKitchen.org (a project of ServiceSpace)
An experiment in generosity in the form of a pay-it-forward restaurant—where there are no prices on the menu, and everyone from the waiter to the dishwasher is a volunteer, and the check at the end of your meal reads $0.00.

KarmaTube.org (a project of ServiceSpace)
Inspiring stories brought to light through the power of video and the Web.

KindSpring.org (a project of ServiceSpace)
A platform dedicated to fostering and celebrating small acts of kindness that change the world.

MovedByLove.org (a project of ServiceSpace)
A volunteer-run space facilitating projects that shift our culture toward a greater sense of trust, connection, and community.

Pledgepage.org (a project of ServiceSpace)
A free online platform for people to showcase and raise funds for their favorite causes.

ProPoor.org (a project of ServiceSpace.org)
An Internet portal that provides information, resources, and news about development work in South Asia.

Story of Stuff Project
www.storyofstuff.org
A community of problem solvers—parents, community leaders, teachers and students, people of faith, entrepreneurs, scientists, and others—working to create a more healthy and just world.

About the Full Bloomers

BAUM, David

Consultant/magician—www.davidbaum.com
"I have been called an organizational travel agent, helping clients figure out where they want to go and getting them there faster."
Read his amazing book *Lightning in a Bottle: Proven Lessons for Leading Change* (Kaplan Publishing, 2000), which is full of energy and insight. It is a delight to read.

BERRY, Duncan

Arc of Light, photography—www.arc-of-light.com
"I have been hunting beauty and meaning in over fifty countries . . . and use this flow of images in my work on climate change solutions and conservation of biologically sensitive lands."
CEO of Fishpeople—www.fishpeopleseafood.com
This sustainable seafood company started from following his Life Map: What do I love? Where are my skills and talents? What does the world need?
Cofounder of Westwind Stewardship Group, an outdoor education organization—www.westwind.org
The land they helped to save now houses an education center providing numerous programs on environmental stewardship.

BERRY, Melany

Event coordinator of Full Heart Productions, musical events and workshops
Tunes in the Dunes and Uke Ohana are inspired events held in Hawaii that came about through her Life Map, blending her love and skills with like-hearted people.
Visit www.tunesinthedunes.com and www.ukeohana.com for more information and to register.

JUDGE, Lita

Artist/author—www.litajudge.net
Lita has a blog and Web site full of delight! Take your time to wander through them.
Her books:
Red Hat (Atheneum Books for Young Readers, 2013)
Bird Talk (Flash Point, 2012)
Red Sled (Atheneum Books for Young Readers, 2011)
Strange Creatures (Disney/Hyperion, 2011)
Born to Be Giants (Flash Point , 2010)
Yellowstone Moran (Viking, 2009)
Pennies for Elephants (Disney/Hyperion, 2009)
One Thousand Tracings: Healing the Wounds of World War II (Hyperion Books for Children, 2007)

MURRAY, Elizabeth

Author, artist, creativity coach, mentor, speaker, workshop leader—www.elizabethmurray.com
Her books:
Cultivating Sacred Space: Gardening for the Soul (Pomegranate, 1997)
Monet's Passion: Ideas, Inspiration and Insights from the Painter's Gardens (Pomegranate, 1989, and the 20th anniversary edition, 2010)
Nantu and Auju: How the Moon and the Potoo Bird Came to Be (Arutam Press, 2004), a trilingual myth from the Achuar people of the rain forest
Painterly Photography: Awakening the Artist Within (Pomegranate, 1993)
Her projects:
Celebrate Beauty—a bimonthly inspirational e-mail; sign up at www.elizabethmurray.com

PECK, Betty

Educator/author—www.annarainville.com
/kindergartenforum.html

Kindergarten Forum—For more than twenty years in Saratoga, California, this has been a highly successful collaboration between Betty Peck and her daughter, Anna Rainville. It is a quarterly series in a magical setting to educate, inspire, and enrich Kindergarten teachers, parents, and administrators in meaningful professional development.

Her books:

Kindergarten Education: Freeing Children's Creative Potential (Hawthorn Press, 2004)

A Kindergarten Teacher Looks at the Word GOD: Reflections on Goodness, Oneness and Diversity (Rudolf Steiner College Press, 2008)

She has two additional books in manuscript form: *Changing All the No's to Yes's and All the Negatives to Positives* and *How to Set Up a Kindergarten Classroom.*

REEVES, Terry

Education director of the Mariposa Museum—www.mariposamuseum.org

A hands-on museum in Peterborough, New Hampshire, showcasing artifacts from around the world and celebrating other cultures with regional exhibitions, performances, and programs.

Terry also works with Children and the Arts Festival, which offers a wide variety of events from puppet making to drumming and so much more. Visit them at www.childrenandthearts.org.

Terry and David Baum's two kids, Galen and Kate, are in Kenya, Africa, working for Free the Children (www.freethechildren.com). The movement was started by a twelve-year-old boy who wanted to end child labor. One of its initiatives is to create systemic change by empowering a generation of active global citizens to change the world on whatever issues they care about. It is one of many organizations David advises.

TWIST, Bill and Lynne

Cofounders of The Pachamama Alliance—www.pachamama.org

Their combined vision is to bring forth an environmentally sustainable, spiritually fulfilling, and socially just human presence on this planet.

They empower indigenous people of the Amazon rain forest to preserve their lands and culture and, using insights gained from that work, educate and inspire individuals everywhere to bring forth a thriving, just, and sustainable world.

Please visit these related Web sites: www.fouryearsgo.org and www.awakenthedreamer.com.

TWIST, Lynne

Global visionary, author, speaker, founder of the Soul of Money Institute—www.lynnetwist.com

Her book:

The Soul of Money: Transforming Your Relationship with Money and Life (W. W. Norton & Company, 2003)

YEH, Lily

Artist—www.barefootartists.org

Founder of the Village of Arts and Humanities—www.villagearts.org

Her book:

Awakening Creativity: Dandelion School Blossoms (New Village Press, 2011)

Her film:

The Barefoot Artist: Be sure to see the clip about Lily's amazing life at www.barefootartistmovie.com.

About the Author

ELIZABETH MURRAY lives a life filled with creativity and joy. Since she was a child, she has been guided by her calling and inspired by Nature, art, and passion. Her photographic images, personal stories, garden metaphors, and humor inspire others to come into Full Bloom as they cultivate their own unique contributions to the garden of life.

In 1985, Elizabeth lived in Monet's gardens in France and assisted in their restoration. Her work inspired her two bestselling books: *Monet's Passion: Ideas, Inspiration, and Insights from the Painter's Gardens* and *Cultivating Sacred Space: Gardening for the Soul.* She makes annual visits to Giverny to photograph the gardens.

Her photographic work is published annually in calendars and is permanently housed in museums and numerous public hospitals, corporations, and private collections in the United States, Europe, and Japan.

Her photography was recently displayed alongside Monet's paintings at the New York Botanical Garden, bringing gardens, art, and spirit of place together for 370,000 visitors. An extensive selection of her Giverny images was chosen to accompany the exhibition *Monet: Late Paintings of Giverny from the Musée Marmottan Monet*, which traveled to seven museums.

Elizabeth paints, draws, and photographs as a joyful meditative practice. Always interested in playful experimentation, she created most of the images for this book with her iPhone and layered apps. She has studied with and been mentored by cultural anthropologist Angeles Arrien, PhD, and Patrick O'Neill, as well as other remarkable wisdom carriers around the world.

She lives in Monterey, California, in a historic redwood home surrounded by beautiful gardens. A keynote speaker and mentor, she offers inspirational workshops and retreats at her home and in locations around the country and the world. Visit her at www.elizabethmurray.com.

Astonished at the beauty,
wonder, and grandeur of Nature,
may we realize our divine
connection and praise and protect
Her on our own path of love,
creation, and service so we can
truly know joy.

Index

Boldfaced page references indicate photographs and illustrations.
Underscored references indicate practice activities.

A

Abrams, David, 83
Achuar people, 15, 25, 46, 78, 85,
    170–72
Action
    examples of, 197
    from passion, 197
    planning for, 194–95
Activism, engaging in, 108, 108
African culture, 60, 176
Afterlife, 76
Alexander, Christopher, 52
Altars, garden, 8
Amazement, discovering radical,
    44, 44
Anam Cara (O'Donohue), 134
Ancestors, honoring, 76, 76
Anderson, Jo, 135
Animals
    bats, 23
    dogs, 77, 115
    learning from, 77, 77
Appreciation, 81
Arrien, Angeles, 57, 60, 60, 81, 87,
    88, 96, 119
Art & Fear (Bayles and Orland), 58
Art, defining, 41
Artist path
    artist's journal, creating,
        43, 43
    artist's state of mind, engaging
        in, 42, 42
    art studio, making, 40, 40
    beauty, celebrating, 45, 45
    body, adorning, 46, 46

community, creating, 47, 47
creative clutter, clearing up,
    48, 48
creativity, igniting, 38–39
dancing, 49, 49
drawing, 41, 41, 51, 51
flowers as art, implementing,
    59, 59
following, 38–39
games, drawing, 51, 51
gardening, 59, 59
healing through art, 52, 52
home, making own art part of,
    53, 53
imagination, igniting, 38–39, 54,
    54
inspiration, developing, 55, 55
knitting, 69, 69
losing self to find self, 56, 56
muses, welcoming, 57, 57
Nature as mentor, opening up
    to, 61, 61
observation, improving, 62, 62
painting, 46, 46, 63, 63
photography, 64, 64
play, incorporating, 65, 65
poetry writing, 66, 66
radical amazement, discovering,
    44, 44
risk of, taking, 67, 67
self-expression, finding courage
    for, 58, 58
sewing, 69, 69
six Ds, remembering, 50, 50

song, finding own, 60, 60
stitching, 69, 69
storytelling, 68, 68
textile art and healing, 69, 69
Artist's journal, creating, 43, 43
Artist's state of mind, engaging in,
    42, 42
Arts and Crafts movement, 53
Art studio, making, 40, 40
Assists, 100
Attentiveness, learning, 25, 25
Authenticity, finding and
    illustrating, 7, 94, 94, 96
Awe, 6

B

Bakhtiar, Jamshid, 116
Balanced Life Map, 198–99, **198**
Basho, Matsuo, 114
Bats, 23
Baum, David, 120, 156–61, **156**, **158**,
    160, **161**, 210
Bayles, David, 58
Beauty, celebrating, 45, 45
Beginning anew, 110, 110
Being present in body, 6
Being present in the moment, 65, 84,
    84, 136
Berry, Duncan, 41, 91, 100, 125, 139,
    162–69, **162**, **165**, **167**, **168**,
    169, 210

Berry, Melany, 125, 162–68, **162, 169**, 210
Big picture, seeing, 128, <u>128</u>
Birds, welcoming, 9, <u>9</u>
Blessings, counting, 81, <u>81</u>, 111, <u>111</u>
Body
    adorning, 46, <u>46</u>
    being present in, 6
    flexible, 93, <u>93</u>
Bol, Gerald (husband of Elizabeth Murray), 98, 114
Breathing
    being present in body and, 6
    in garden, 6, <u>6</u>, 10, <u>10</u>
    for relaxation, 10, <u>10</u>
Buddha, 14, 20
Buddhism, 115, 117
Burgy, Kathleen, 79, 97, 130
Butterflies, transformation, and self, 11, <u>11</u>

C

Calling in life
    finding, 74, <u>74</u>
    following, 137, <u>137</u>
Cameras, 64, <u>64</u>
Cameron, Jeanne, 59
Campbell, Joseph, 74
Castaneda, Carlos, 62
Celebration, creating, 112, <u>112</u>
Celtic culture, 53–54
Chi (life energy), 35, 98
Children
    in garden, inviting, 12, <u>12</u>
    gift of, 78
    mud kisses and, making, 12
    nurturing, 78, <u>78</u>
    Peck (Betty) and, 142–46
    playing like, 22, <u>22</u>
    Reeves and, 158
    storytelling and, <u>68</u>

Clarity and depth, seeing with, 91, <u>91</u>, 127
Cline, Kay, 132
Commitment bundles, making, 87, <u>87</u>
Commitment, making, 85, <u>85</u>, 87, <u>87</u>
Communication, working at, 88, <u>88</u>
Community
    creating, 47, <u>47</u>
    dreams, listening to, 116
    finding own, 134–35, <u>134</u>
Compassion for self, finding, 113, <u>113</u>
Composting soil, 27
Confidence, 94
Connections, finding, 193–94
Cook, Eliza, 19
Courage
    finding, 89, <u>89</u>
    importance of, 89
    for risk-taking, 67
    for self-expression, 58, <u>58</u>
Create (universal force), 119
Creative clutter, clearing up, 48, <u>48</u>
Creativity, igniting, 38–39
Curiosity, acting on, 90, <u>90</u>

D

Dali Lama, 17
Dancing, 49, <u>49</u>
Dawn, greeting, 15, <u>15</u>
Daydreams, listening to, 116
Death, dealing with, 114–15, <u>114</u>
Decluttering, 48, <u>48</u>
Dedication, 50
Deep listening, 97, <u>97</u>
Delight, 50
Depth and clarity, seeing with, 91, <u>91</u>, 127
Desire, 50
Determination, 50

Devotion, 50
Discipline, 50
Dogs, 77, 115
Doing what you love, 86, <u>86</u>
Dotson, John, 66
Drawing, 41, <u>41</u>, 51, <u>51</u>
Dreams, listening to nighttime, 116, <u>116</u>

E

Elders, embracing, 79, <u>79</u>
Encouragement, giving to others, 89, <u>89</u>
Endorphins, 26, 82
Environmental stewardship, 164–68
Ephemeral art. *See specific type*

F

Fairy mailbox, creating, 13, <u>13</u>
Family, treasuring, 92, <u>92</u>
Fear, paralysis of, 58
Fenton (uncle of Elizabeth Murray), 64, 68, 79
Five universal forces, integrating, 119, <u>119</u>
Flexibility in mind and body, achieving, 93, <u>93</u>
Flowers. *See also* Plants
    as art, implementing, 59, <u>59</u>
    beauty of, admiring, 14, <u>14</u>
    body adornment and, 46, <u>46</u>
    lotus, open to being, 124, <u>124</u>
    metaphor of, <u>14</u>
    nasturtiums, 24
    rock rose, 14
Food, savoring with gratitude, 16, <u>16</u>
Forgiveness, extending, <u>82</u>, 102, <u>102</u>
Fort Ord, 132

Four pathways. *See also* Artist path; Full Bloomers; Gardener path; Lover path; Spirit-Weaver path
  following, 1, 185
  inspiration in, finding, 196
  reflecting on, 188
Fox, Matthew, 44
French culture, 129
Friendships, cherishing, 80, <u>80</u>
Full Bloomers
  Baum, David, 120, 156–61, **156, 158, 160, 161**, 210
  Berry, Duncan, 41, 91, 100, 125, 139, 162–68, **162, 165, 167, 168, 169**, 210
  Berry, Melany, 125, 162–68, **162, 169**, 210
  describing, 141
  Judge, Lita, 43, 52, 57, 150–55, **150, 151, 152**, 210
  Murray, Elizabeth, 210–11
  Peck, Betty, 12, 142–49, **142, 145, 147, 148**, 211
  Reeves, Terry, 156–61, **156, 158**, 211
  Twist, Bill, 170–75, **170**, 211
  Twist, Lynne, 81, 170–75, **170, 175**, 211
  Yeh, Lily, 176–83, **176, 178, 179, 183**, 211
Fuller, Buckminster, 128
Fuller, Thomas, 35

G
Games, drawing, 51, <u>51</u>
Gardener path
  attentiveness, learning, 25, <u>25</u>
  birds, welcoming, 9, <u>9</u>
  breathing, 6, <u>6</u>, 10, <u>10</u>
  butterflies, transformation, and self, 11, <u>11</u>
  children in garden, inviting, 12, <u>12</u>
  dawn, greeting, 15, <u>15</u>
  fairy mailbox, creating, 13, <u>13</u>
  flowers' beauty, admiring, 14, <u>14</u>
  following, 4–5
  food, savoring with gratitude, 16, <u>16</u>
  garden paths, walking, 20, <u>20</u>
  generosity, promoting, 31, <u>31</u>
  herbs, planting, 18, <u>18</u>
  home, creating, 19, <u>19</u>
  Japanese beauty, embracing essence of, 34, <u>34</u>
  night, embracing, 30, <u>30</u>
  patience, learning, 25, <u>25</u>
  permaculture, learning from, 21, <u>21</u>
  plant vibrations, feeling, 33, <u>33</u>
  playing like child, 22, <u>22</u>
  pollinating plants, 23, <u>23</u>
  purposeful happiness, finding, 17, <u>17</u>
  sacred space, creating, 8, <u>8</u>
  seeds, planting, 24, <u>24</u>
  senses, awakening, 26, <u>26</u>
  sky, being aware of, 28, <u>28</u>
  soil and soul, connection between, 27, <u>27</u>
  spirit of place, respecting, 29, <u>29</u>
  trees, gleaning wisdom from, 32, <u>32</u>
  water, conserving, 35, <u>35</u>
  wildness within, finding, 7, <u>7</u>
Gardening as art form, 59, <u>59</u>
Garden paths, walking, 20, <u>20</u>
Gatha, creating, 139, <u>139</u>
Gathering of Nations Pow Wow, 92
Generosity, promoting, 31, <u>31</u>, 117, <u>117</u>
Genius loci, respecting, 29, <u>29</u>
Giving to others, 117, <u>117</u>
Gratitude, 16, 81

Green Belt Movement, 32
Gröner, Thomas, 59

H
Hafiz, 58, 66
Haida Gwaii, 31
Hall, Arthur, 176
Hamlet (Shakespeare character), 18
Happiness
  knowing own, 118, <u>118</u>
  purposeful, finding, 17, <u>17</u>
Harmon, Jay, 61
Harvey, Andrew, 108
Healing
  through art, 52, <u>52</u>
  flowers and, 14
  through humor, 120, <u>120</u>
  through textile art, 69, <u>69</u>
  as universal force, 119
Hemingway, Ernest, 89
Herbs, planting, 18, <u>18</u>
Hidden Beauty, The (film), <u>23</u>
Holmes, Mary, 56
Home
  creating, 19, <u>19</u>
  making own art part of, 53, <u>53</u>
Honeybees, 23
Houston, Jean, 133
Hubbard, Barbara Marx, 122
Humor, healing power of, 120, <u>120</u>

I
Illness, cultivating intimacy during, 96
Imagination, igniting, 38–39, 54, <u>54</u>
Impermanence, dealing with, 114–15, <u>114</u>
Initiate (universal force), 119
Insight, instantaneous flash of, 55

Inspiration, developing, 55, 55
Integrate (universal force), 119
Integrity, 94
Intimacy
    cultivating personal, 96, 96
    with the land, 61
Intuition, trusting in, 121, 121

J

Japanese beauty, embracing
    essence of, 34, 34
Jarvis, Ed, 57
Joie de vivre, 129, 129
Joy, path to, 186
Judge, Dave, 150–51, 153–55
Judge, Lita, 43, 52, 57, 150–55, **150,**
    151, 152, 210

K

"Kindergarten Teacher's Creed,
    The" (Betty Peck), 149
Kindness, showing, 82, 82
King, Martin Luther, 116
Knitting, 69, 69
Knitting Behind Bars program, 69

L

Labyrinths, 20, 110
Lao Tzu, 24
Laughter, engaging in, 120, 120
Leadership, learning, 122, 122
Life energy, 35, 98
Life Map
    action, planning for, 194–95
    balanced, 198–99, **198**
    circles, filling in, 193
    connections, finding, 193–94

creating, 192–96, **192**
depth and clarity and, 91
example of, **187**
first, 90
function of, 186
materials for, 188
North Star and, finding personal,
    186, 195–96
overview of, 186
passions and, 189
personal story and, exploring,
    188
skills and, 190, 190
talents and, 190, 190
world's needs and, 191, 191
Light
    following, 123, 123
    in garden, 28
Listening, deep, 97, 97
Living in Gratitude (Arrien), 81
Longfellow, Henry Wadsworth, 61
Losing self to find self, 56, 56
Lotus, open to being, 124, 124
Love
    commitment to, 85, 85
    as compass in life, 86, 86, 103
    of self, developing, 103, 103
Lover path
    ancestors, honoring, 76, 76
    animals, learning from, 77, 77
    authenticity, illustrating, 94, 94
    being present in the moment,
        84, 84
    calling in life, finding, 74, 74
    children, nurturing, 78, 78
    commitment, making, 85, 85,
        87, 87
    communication, working at, 88, 88
    courage, finding, 89, 89
    curiosity, acting on, 90, 90
    depth and clarity, seeing with,
        91, 91
    doing what you love, 86, 86
    elders, embracing, 79, 79

encouragement, giving to others,
    89, 89
family, treasuring, 92, 92
flexibility in mind and body,
    achieving, 93, 93
following, 72–73
forgiveness, extending, 102, 102
friendships, cherishing, 80, 80
intimacy, cultivating personal,
    96, 96
kindness, showing, 82, 82
listening, deep, 97, 97
love as compass in life, 86, 86
nature, falling in love with, 83, 83
passion for place, sharing, 99, 99
passions, finding, 75, 75
self-love, developing, 103, 103
service, engaging in, 100, 100
spirit, finding, 98, 98
sufficiency, cultivating, 101, 101
thanks, giving, 81, 81
vulnerability, letting in, 95, 95

M

Maathai, Wangari, 32
Macy, Joanna, 122, 165
Matisse, Henri, 51, 63
Maturation, 109, 109
McKeon, Margot, 82
Meandering garden paths, 20
Meditation, engaging in, 125, 125
Mellon, Nancy, 68
Mentors, finding, 61, 61, 126, 126
Metamorphosis. *See*
    Transformation, personal
Mind
    flexible, 93, 93
    presence of, 127, 127
Mindfulness, developing, 127, 127
Mitchell, Edgar, 128
Moment, being present in, 65, 84,
    84, 136

Monet, Claude, 19, 28, 44, 52, 61, 122
Monet's (Claude) garden, 20, 24, 33, 52, 124
Moon's phases, 30
Moore, Margaret, 69
Moore, Thomas, 130
Morris, William, 53
Mud, emerging from, 124, 124
Mud kisses, making, 12
Murray, Elizabeth, 210–13
Mursi people, 46
Muses, welcoming, 57, 57
Music, 60, 60
Musset, Alfred de, 66

N

Nasturtiums, 24
Nature. Beauty. Gratitude (film), 81
Nature
    connection to, human, 128
    falling in love with, 83, 83
    lessons from, learning, 21
    light and, 123
    as mentor, opening up to, 61, 61
Navajo blessing, 45
Nearing, Scott, 44
New life purpose, discovering, 110, 110
Night, embracing, 30, 30
Nighttime dreams, listening to, 15, 116, 116
Nin, Anaïs, 124
Nine Muses, The (Arrien), 57
North Star, finding personal, 186, 195–96
"No time presence," 42

O

Observation, improving, 61–62, 62
O'Donohue, John, 54, 111, 134
O'Neill, Patrick, 88, 88
Orland, Ted, 58
Overview (film), 128
"Overview effect," 128
Oxytocin, 112

P

Pacific Northwest natives, 31
Painting, 46, 46, 63, 63
Pam (sister-in-law of Elizabeth Murray), 84, 114
Passion
    action from, 197
    finding, 75, 75
    Life Map and, 189
    for place, sharing, 99, 99
    seed words for, 189
Patience, learning, 25, 25
Peach, becoming, 109, 109
Peck, Betty, 12, 142–49, 142, 145, 147, 148, 211
Peck, Willys, 142, 144–45, 147–48
Permaculture, learning from, 21, 21
Personal story, exploring, 188
Pets, 77, 115
Philanthropy, 117
Photography, 64, 64
Place
    passion for, sharing, 99, 99
    spirit of, respecting, 29, 29
Plants. See also Flowers; Trees
    herbs, 18, 18
    pollinating, 23, 23
    vibrations of, feeling, 33, 33
Plato, 33

Play
    in art, incorporating in general, 65, 65
    child's, 22, 22
    in drawing, 51, 51
    remembering to, 65, 65
Poetry writing, 66, 66
Pollinating plants, 23, 23
Potlach, 31
Practices for Artist path
    artist's journal, creating, 43
    artist's state of mind, engaging in, 42
    art studio, making, 40
    beauty, celebrating, 45
    body, adorning, 46
    community, creating, 47
    creative clutter, clearing up, 48
    dancing, 49
    drawing, 41, 51
    flowers as art, implementing, 59
    games, drawing, 51
    gardening, 59
    healing through art, 52
    home, making own art part of, 53
    imagination, igniting, 54
    inspiration, developing, 55
    knitting, 69
    losing self to find self, 56
    muses, welcoming, 57
    nature as mentor, opening up to, 61
    observation, improving, 62
    painting, 46, 63
    photography, 64
    play, incorporating, 65
    poetry writing, 66
    radical amazement, discovering, 44
    risk of, taking, 67
    self-expression, finding courage for, 58
    sewing, 69
    six Ds, remembering, 50

song, finding own, 60
stitching, 69
storytelling, 68
textile art and healing, 69
Practices for Gardener path
  attentiveness, learning, 25
  birds, welcoming, 9
  breathing, 6, 10
  butterflies, transformation, and
    self, 11
  children in garden, inviting, 12
  dawn, greeting, 15
  fairy mailbox, creating, 13
  flowers' beauty, admiring, 14
  food, savoring with gratitude, 16
  garden paths, walking, 20
  generosity, promoting, 31
  herbs, planting, 18
  home, creating, 19
  Japanese beauty, embracing
    essence of, 34
  night, embracing, 30
  patience, learning, 25
  permaculture, learning from, 21
  plant vibrations, feeling, 33
  playing like a child, 22
  pollinating plants, 23
  purposeful happiness, finding, 17
  sacred space, creating, 8
  seeds, planting, 24
  senses, awakening, 26
  sky, being aware of, 28
  soil and soul, connection
    between, 27
  spirit of place, respecting, 29
  trees, gleaning wisdom from, 32
  water, conserving, 35
  wildness within, finding, 7
Practices for Lover path
  ancestors, honoring, 76
  animals, learning from, 77
  authenticity, illustrating, 94
  being present in the moment, 84
  calling in life, finding, 74

children, nurturing, 78
commitment, making, 85, 87
communication, working at, 88
courage, finding, 89
curiosity, acting on, 90
depth and clarity, seeing with, 91
doing what you love, 86
elders, embracing, 79
encouragement, giving to
  others, 89
family, treasuring, 92
flexibility in mind and body,
  achieving, 93
forgiveness, extending, 102
friendships, cherishing, 80
intimacy, cultivating personal, 96
kindness, showing, 82
listening, deep, 97
love as compass in life, 86
Nature, falling in love with, 83
passion for place, sharing, 99
passions, finding, 75
self-love, developing, 103
service, engaging in, 100
spirit, finding, 98
sufficiency, cultivating, 101
thanks, giving, 81
vulnerability, letting in, 95
Practices for Spirit-Weaver path
  activism, engaging in, 108
  beginning anew, 110
  big picture, seeing, 128
  blessings, counting, 111
  calling in life, following, 137
  celebration, creating, 112
  community, finding own, 134
  compassion for self, finding, 113
  death, dealing with, 114
  gatha, creating, 139
  generosity, promoting, 117
  giving to others, 117
  happiness, knowing own, 118
  humor, healing power of, 120
  impermanence, dealing with, 114

intuition, trusting in, 121
leadership, learning, 122
light, following, 123
lotus, open to being, 124
meditation, engaging in, 125
mentors, finding, 126
mindfulness, developing, 127
mud, emerging from, 124
new life purpose, discovering,
  110
nighttime dreams, listening
  to, 116
Peach, becoming, 109
prayer, engaging in, 125
rituals, creating, 112
sabbath, observing own, 129
silence, giving self the gift of, 130
simplicity, enriching own life
  with, 131
soul, developing relationship
  with, 133
stewardship, engaging in, 132
time, enjoying, 136
tribe, finding own, 134
universal forces, integrating
  five, 119
wisdom, gaining, 109
Wisdom-Keeper, becoming, 138
Prayer, engaging in, 125, 125
Proverbs, 16
Psalms, 79
Purposeful happiness, finding, 17, 17
Purposeful living, engaging in,
  74, 74

Quakers, 88, 97
Quotations
  Basho, Matsuo, 114
  Berry, Duncan, 169
  Buddha, 14, 20

Quotations (*cont.*)
  Cook, Eliza, 19
  Fox, Matthew, 107
  Fuller, Thomas, 35
  Hafiz, 58
  Hamlet, 18
  Judge, Lita, 155
  Lao Tzu, 24
  Longfellow, Henry Wadsworth,
    61
  McKeon, Margot, 82
  Musset, Alfred de, 66
  Plato, 33
  Proverbs, 16
  Psalms, 79
  Rodale, Bob, 27
  Rumi, 60
  Tao Te Ching, 73
  Thich Nhat Hanh, 5
  Thoreau, Henry David, 15, 116
  Twist, Lynne, 175

R

Radiant Coat, The, 79
Radical amazement, discovering,
  44, 44
Reeves, Terry, 156–61, **156**, **158**, 211
Relatives, treasuring, 92, 92
Relaxation, 10, 10, 125, 125
Religion
  Buddhism, 115, 117
  generosity and, 117
Rendlen, Branham, 42
Resources
  books, 204–5
  films and videos, 206
  organizations, 206
  people, 206
  service portals, 209
  Ted Talks, 207
  Web sites, 207–9

Reynolds, Dana, 43
"Right livelihood," 162
"Right relationship," 88
Risk of Artist path, taking, 67, 67
Rituals, creating, 112, 112, 123
Rock rose, 14
Rodale, Bob, 27
Roosevelt, Teddy, 9
Rosemary (herb), 18
Rumi, 60, 86

S

Sabbath, observing own, 129,
  129
Sabi concept, embracing, 34, 34
Sacred activism, 108
Sacred space, creating and sharing,
  8, 8, 22
Schwartzberg, Louie, 23, 81
Seeds, planting, 24, 24
Seed words
  for passions, 189
  for skills and talents, 190
  for world's needs, 191
Self-doubt, 67
Self-expression, finding courage
  for, 58, 58
Self-love, developing, 103, 103
Senses, awakening, 26, 26
Service, engaging in, 100, 100
Sewing, 69, 69
Silence, giving self the gift of,
  130, 130
Simplicity, enriching own life with,
  131, 131
Singing in garden, 25
Six Ds, remembering, 50, 50
Skills, 190, 190, 197
Sky
  being aware of, 28, 28
  night, embracing, 30, 30

Soil
  composting, 27
  soul and, connection between,
    27, 27
Song, finding own, 60, 60
Soul
  relationship with, developing,
    133, 133
  soil and, connection between,
    27, 27
Sound vibrations, 33, 33
Spiral garden paths, 20
Spirit
  in all beings, believing in, 76
  finding own, 98, 98
  of place, respecting, 29, 29
Spirit-Weaver path
  activism, engaging in, 108, 108
  beginning anew, 110, 110
  big picture, seeing, 128, 128
  blessings, counting, 111, 111
  calling in life, following, 137, 137
  celebration, creating, 112, 112
  community, finding own,
    134–35, 134
  compassion for self, finding,
    113, 113
  death, dealing with, 114–15, 114
  following, 106–7
  gatha, creating, 139, 139
  generosity, promoting, 117, 117
  giving to others, 117, 117
  happiness, knowing own, 118, 118
  humor, healing power of, 120, 120
  impermanence, dealing with,
    114–15, 114
  intuition, trusting in, 121, 121
  leadership, learning, 122, 122
  light, following, 123, 123
  lotus, open to being, 124, 124
  meditation, engaging in, 125, 125
  mentors, finding, 126, 126
  mindfulness, developing, 127, 127
  mud, emerging from, 124, 124

new life purpose, discovering, 110, 110
nighttime dreams, listening to, 116, 116
Peach, becoming, 109, 109
prayer, engaging in, 125, 125
rituals, creating, 112, 112
sabbath, observing own, 129, 129
silence, giving self the gift of, 130, 130
simplicity, enriching own life with, 131, 131
soul, developing relationship with, 133, 133
stewardship, engaging in, 132, 132
time, enjoying, 136, 136
tribe, finding own, 134–35, 134
universal forces, integrating five, 119, 119
wisdom, gaining, 109, 109
Wisdom Keeper, becoming, 138, 138
Stars, watching, 30, 30
Steindl-Rast, David, 81
Stewardship
  engaging in, 132, 132
  environmental, 164–68
Stitching, 69, 69
Story of Stuff, The (video), 131
Storytelling, 68, 68
Straight garden paths, 20
Sufficiency, cultivating, 101, 101
Suki concept, embracing, 34, 34
Surma people, 46
Sutton-Smith, Brian, 65
Swimme, Brian, 30

Talents, 190, 190, 197
Tao Te Ching, 73

Teilhard de Chardin, Pierre, 75, 135
Ten Perfections, 117
Teresa, Mother, 100
Textile art for healing, 69, 69
Thanks, giving, 81, 81
Thich Nhat Hanh, 5
Thomas (brother of Elizabeth Murray), 62
Thoreau, Henry David, 15, 116
Time, enjoying, 136, 136
Timeless Way of Building, The (Alexander), 52
To Bless the Space Between Us (O'Donohue), 111
Toolie (dog of Elizabeth Murray), 77, 115
Totem poles, 31
Transform (universal force), 119
Transformation, personal, 11, 11, 199
Trees, gleaning wisdom from, 32, 32
Tribe, finding own, 134–35, 134
Twa people, 181
Twist, Bill, 170–75, **170**, 211
Twist, Lynne, 81, 170–75, **170**, **175**, 211

Universal forces, integrating five, 119, 119

Via creativa, 44
Via positiva, 44
Vibrations in garden, 33, 33
"Views to Healing," 52
Vocation, 137
Vulnerability, letting in, 95, 95

Wabi concept, embracing, 34, 34
"Walking in Beauty" (Navajo blessing), 45
Water, conserving, 35, 35
White, Frank, 128
Whyte, David, 66
Wildness within, finding, 7, 7
Williams, Terry Tempest, 182
Wisdom, gaining and sharing, 109, 109, 138
Wisdom Keeper, becoming, 138, 138
World's needs, 191, 191, 197

Yeh, Lily, 176–83, **176**, **178**, **179**, **183**, 211

Zen meditation gardens, 41
Zen sticky notes, creating, 139, 139